NATIONAL MUSEUM OF ANTHROPOLOGY

OFFICIAL GUIDE

NATIONAL MUSEUM OF ANTHROPOLOGY

TEXTS

Archaeology:
Carolin Baus de Czitrom, Rosa Margarita Brambila Paz, Amalia Cardós de Méndez, Martha Carmona Macías, Marcia Castro-Leal Espino, Ma. Dolores Flores Villatoro, Ma. Teresa García García, Ma. de la Cruz Paillés H., Federica Sodi Miranda, Felipe R. Solís Olguín, Olivia Torres Cabello y Margarita Velasco Mireles,

Ethnography:
Efraín Cortés Ruiz, Ma. Olimpia Farfán Morales, Jorge Gómez Poncet, Donaciano Gutiérrez Gutiérrez, Beatriz M. Oliver Vega, Dora Sierra Carrillo, Ma. Cristina Suárez y Farías y Plácido Villanueva Peredo.

INAH–SALVAT

NATIONAL INSTITUTE OF ANTHROPOLOGY AND HISTORY

GENERAL DIRECTOR
Arqlgo. Roberto García Moll

MUSEUMS AND EXHIBITIONS ADMINISTRATION
Mario Vázquez Ruvalcaba

NATIONAL DIFUSION ADMINISTRATION
Jaime Bali Wuest

PUBLICATIONS ADMINISTRATION
Antonio Guzmán Vázquez

ANTHROPOLOGY MUSEUM ADMINISTRATION
Dra. Mari Carmen Serra Puche

SALVAT EDITORES DE MEXICO

EDITORIAL COORDINATOR
Ma. Guadalupe Casillas

DESIGN AND ILLUSTRATIONS
Carlos Anaya
Sergio Arzate
Patricia Rubio

PHOTOGRAPHY
Alejandro Mass
Archivo Salvat

PLANS OF ARCHEOLOGY SECTION
Eduardo Hernández Pérez

TRANSLATION
Helen Jones Perrott de Mandri

1987 First edition
1988 First reimpression
1989 Second reimpression
1990 Third reimpression
1991 Fourth reimpression
1991 Fifth reimpression

PRINTED IN 1991 BY
Gráficas Monte Albán, S.A. de C.V.
Municipio El Marqués, Querétaro

Impreso en México
Printed in Mexico

Index

General Information

Location

The National Anthropology Museum is situated in the first section of Chapultepec Park along Paseo de la Reforma, adjoining Gandhi Street. The site was chosen for its historical importance.

The main entrance to visit the Museum is located on Reforma near the monument dedicated to the god Tláloc.

Visiting Hours

The Museum is open to the public from Tuesday to Saturday from 9:00 to 19:00 hours; Sundays and holidays from 10:00 to 18:00 hours. Tickets cost 800 pesos, except on Sundays and holidays, when entrance is free of charge. The fee includes a view of the permanent exhibition halls containing the archaeological collections, with the ethnographic section upstairs. Students of private schools affiliated to CREA and CONACURT pay half price. Children under 12, indigenous groups, invalids, INSEN associates and uniformed government officials may enter free of charge.

Organization

The Museum contains the Head Office of the Museum, the Administration, the General Office, the Archaeology, Ethnography and Museography departments, Educational Services, Guided Tours, Public Relations and Publicity. It also contains workshops, laboratories, study storerooms and investigation studios.

The building also houses departments of Physical Anthropology, Linguistics, Sub-aquatic Archaeology and Ethnography and a section of Electronic Machinery. Furthermore, the National Library of Anthropology and History is also in this building.

Guided Tours

The Museum has a team of guides who speak various languages, such as French, German and English. The tour in Spanish is free of charge but there is a small fee of 500 pesos for the tour in other languages. If a tour for a certain number of people is required on a certain day at a specific time, it would be advisable to book by telephone at the following number: 553-6266 extensions 24 and 25.

Educational Services

Through the Educational Services Department, the Museum offers a guided tour for children appropriate to their scholastic level. During the vacation periods there are summer workshops which include basic elements of engraving, painting, modelling, folk dancing etc. It also offers courses in ethnographic material for teachers. Telephones: 553-6266 extensions 65 and 67.

Orientation Room

There is an Orientation room in the vestibule of the Museum where the visitor can obtain an overall view of the contents of the Museum by an audio visual system.

Publicity Department

This department is in charge of organizing exhibitions, conferences of an anthropological nature, a series of talks to become acquainted with the Museum called "Visit the Museum with us", and organizing, promoting and publicizing cultural activities.

Library

The reading rooms of the library are open from Monday to Friday from 9:00 to 20:45 hours; Saturdays from 9:00 to 13:00 hours and Sundays from 8:30 to 13:00 hours. Some of the services offered in the Library have a special timetable. Among these special services are the possibility of lending material within the building and outside; consultancy and reference services; audiovisual material, micro-film archives, language library, map library, transparency library, oral history archives, pictoric records (códices); serial newspaper and journal publications; reading rooms; reproductions and photocopies; bibliography bulletin; etcetera.

Special Services

Temporary exhibitions, round tables, monthly exhibit, restaurant, infirmary, wheel chairs and lending of auditoriums for cultural activities; for the latter service one should consult the Administration Department of the Museum.

Note

The pieces shown with an asterisk were removed from the Museum on December 25, 1985.

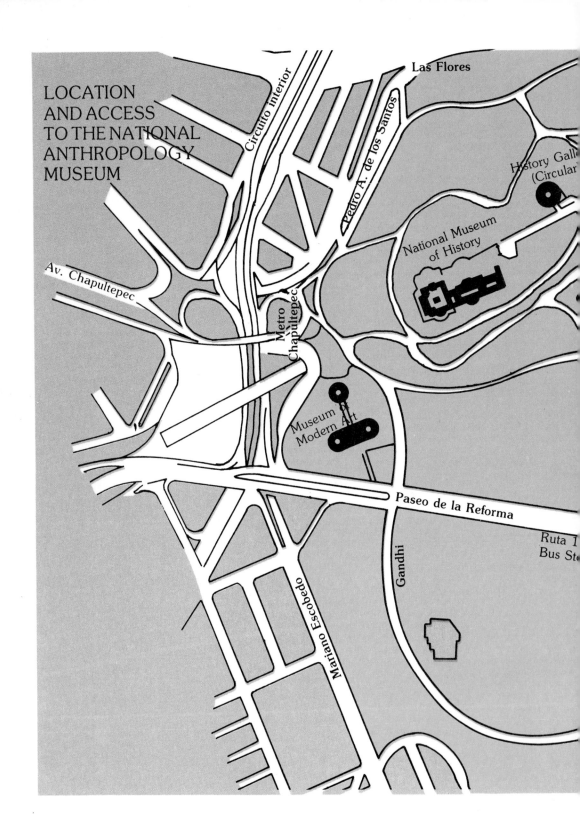

LOCATION
AND ACCESS
TO THE NATIONAL
ANTHROPOLOGY
MUSEUM

Las Flores

Circuito Interior

Pedro A. de los Santos

History Gall
(Circular

National Museum
of History

Av. Chapultepec

Metro
Chapultepec

Museum of
Modern Art

Paseo de la Reforma

Mariano Escobedo

Gandhi

Ruta 1
Bus Ste

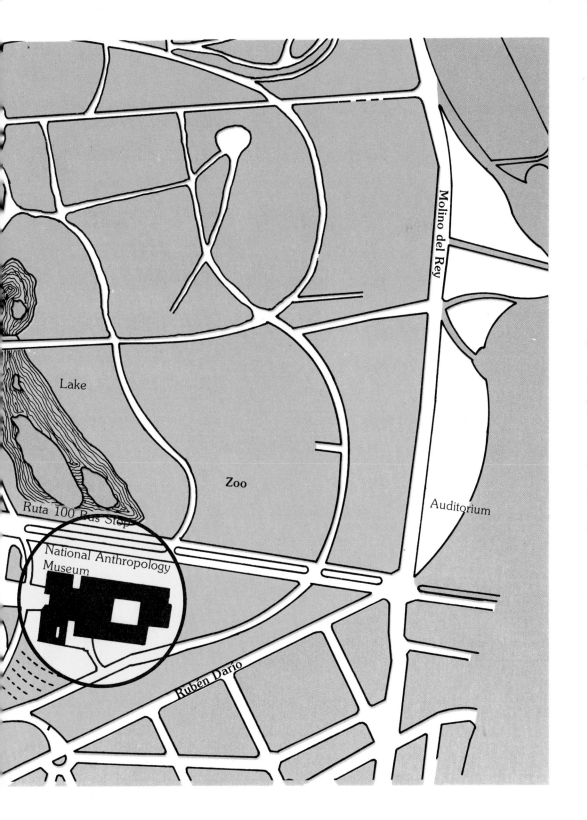

INTRODUCTION

THE NATIONAL MUSEUM

The National Museum was the first of its kind on the American continent when an edict to form the Institution was signed on March 18th, 1825. At that time, the building was located in the Royal Pontifical University of Mexico and was divided in two main sections, —antiquities and natural history.

During the nineteenth century, the Museum was one of the most important places to visit in Mexico City. It was open to the public on Tuesdays, Thursdays and Saturdays and operated on a budget between $8,800 and $12,000 pesos.

A decree for the definite formalization of the Museum was issued in 1831. It was to be divided in three sections which included antiquities, industrial products and the third section combined natural history with a botanical garden. However, it still did not have a special building allocated for the purpose.

By a Presidential decree on March 18, 1825 of Guadalupe Victoria, the first *National Mexican Museum* was formed in one of the lecture halls of the Old University.

México Pintoresco. = La ex-Universidad.

La antigua Universidad, hoy Conservatorio de Música

EL MUSEO NACIONAL.
La vista comprende la calle de la Moneda.

The Museum in the Exchange Building 1866-1964

On July 6th, 1866, the Museum was transferred to the Exchange Building near the National Palace, where it remained until September 1964. It was known as the Public Museum of Natural History, Archaeology and History, and was open to the public for two hours every Tuesday, Thursday and Sunday.

In 1867 its name was changed back to the National Museum and by 1877 a library was opened to the public which is still in use today. In 1855, the Stone of the Sun was found in one of the towers of the City cathedral and was taken to the Museum. This piece may now be found in the Mexica Hall of the present Museum.

The Physical Anthropology and Ethnography section, Comparative Anatomy, Applied Zoology and Botany sections and the Monolith Gallery were inaugurated by the President at the time, Porfirio Díaz, in 1887.

In the same year, the Museum organized the first scientific archaeological expedition to Oaxaca. Another was organized to Veracruz in 1890, both under the guidance of the well-known historian Francisco del Paso y Troncoso.

In 1866 the Public Museum of Natural History, Archaeology and History was housed in the *Old Mint* buildings. The following year the museum changed its name to the National Museum.

11

The 1890 expedition to Zempoala, Veracruz, marked the recognition of the Museum as a dynamic instrument in the recuperation of the nation's archaeological heritage. The year 1892 marked the same promotion in the field of ethnography, when the first expedition of its kind was organized to collect ethnographic material throughout the country, to send to Madrid for an exhibition that commemorated the fourth centenary of the discovery of America.

In 1893, the Museum also conducted investigations into the indigenous languages and helped to preserve some dialects which were fast disappearing. In this way the Museum covered all branches of anthropology: archaeology, ethnography, physical anthropology and linguistics.

The National Museum was already giving archaeology, history, ethnology and náhuatl classes in 1905 and by 1907 explanatory notes were placed beneath the objects to give better information to the public.

In 1909 the National Museum was separated from the Natural History collection, which was housed in El Chopo Building. It was then called the National Museum of Archaeology, History and Ethnography. In the following year the Museum was reorganized and by 1911 also housed the International School of American Archaeology and Ethnography, where intellectuals from all over the world collaborated with work lecture courses.

An important aspect of the Museum was its publication of various papers and treaties and by 1912 some books had been published, some of them receiving international prizes and recognition.

Until 1939, the year in which the National Anthropology Institute and the National Museum were formed, it was the most important historical and anthropological center in the country. This was the year in which the historical collection was separated and transferred to the recently created National History Museum in Chapultepec Castle. The remaining collection was then renamed the National Museum of Anthropology.

After 1939 it formed part of the National Institute of Anthropology and History and continued to attract the most outstanding anthropologists and historians of the time. Furthermore it was a center for research, conservation and display, as well as teaching courses on anthropology that included archaeology and linguistics.

The National School of Anthropology and History was founded in 1941 and remained there until 1970. The Exchange Building had among its exhibits on display, mainly archaeological and ethnographic material, but it also contained research departments and a library for public use.

The important role that this institute, known by various names at different times: Mexican, Public Natural History, History and Archaeology, History and Ethnography and finally National Anthropology, has played in the preservation, study and diffusion of our national heritage, is little known, but it was the Museum that was the first institute to concern itself with those aspects which form our national identity.

The archaeological collections were from the first, amongst the most important and included exhibits from Sacrifice Island, Veracruz, the monoliths donated by Diego de la Rosa, other donations from Sama, Plancarte, Heredia, Seler etc., and the many other exhibits that have been collected little by little, throughout the 154 years of the Museum's existence. All these collections have remained as indelible proofs in the history of the National Museum and of Mexican archaeology.

For more than a hundred years the Museum remained as the main center for Mexican history and anthropological research. Without doubt, much of the prehispanic art and ethnography, now seen by generations of Mexicans, would have been lost without the existence of the Museum.

View of the *Museum's central patio*, taken from outside the Mexica Hall.

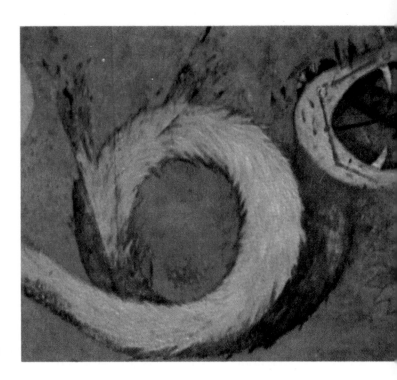

Day and Night, mural painting by Rufino Tamayo.

The New Building in Chapultepec-1964

The present National Museum of Anthropology is located in the first section of Chapultepec Park. Designed by the architect Pedro Ramírez Vázquez, it was built in eighteen months with the help of a large team of people which included 42 engineers, 52 architects, 40 scientific advisors, anthropologists, historians, educational assistants, painters and sculptors. The inauguration took place on September 17th 1964.

The Museum has 30,000 square meters of exhibition space, 6,000 dedicated to workshops, laboratories and storerooms and 45,000 square meters of open areas.

There are 24 permanent exhibition halls in 28,900 square meters and 1,400 square meters for temporary exhibitions, with three auditoriums with seating capacity for a total of 630 people. It also houses the "Eusebio Dávalos Hurtado" Library of the National Institute of Anthropology and History, with a capacity for 50,000 volumes. For some years now, it has also included the National Anthropology and History School, with capacity for 500 students.

Furthermore, various research departments operate from the Museum such as: Linguistics, Underwater Archaeology,

Ethnohistory, Physical Anthropology, Archives and Libraries of the National Institute of Anthropology and History. The Institute's Cultural Tours Departament is also found on the ground floor.

In the Orientations Room found in the entrance hall, the visitor can gain an idea of the Museum's contents from an audio-visual explanation with scale models. There is also a hall for temporary exhibits to the right of the main entrance.

The pillar supporting the roof of the patio is the design of the Chávez Morado brothers. It covers an area of 4, 368 square meters at a height of 28.70 meters and weighs 2,000 tons.

There are various paintings and murals dispersed throughout the exhibition halls, which were executed by the following artists: Raúl Anguiano, Leonora Carrington, Rafael Coronel, Luis Covarrubias, José Chávez Morado, Arturo García Bustos, Matias Goeritz, Jorge González Camarena, Rina Lazo, Carlos Mérida, Adolfo Mexiac, Pablo O'Higgins, Fanny Rabel, Regina Roull, Rufino Tamayo and Agustín Villagra.

GROUND FLOOR PLAN

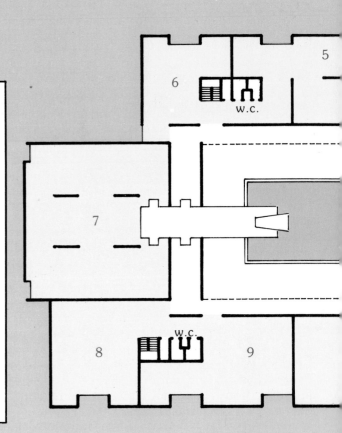

Halls

1 Introduction to Anthropology
2 Mesoamerica
3 Origins
4 Preclassic
5 Teotihuacan
6 Toltec
7 Mexica
8 Oaxaca
9 Gulf Coast
10 Maya
11 North of Mexico
12 West

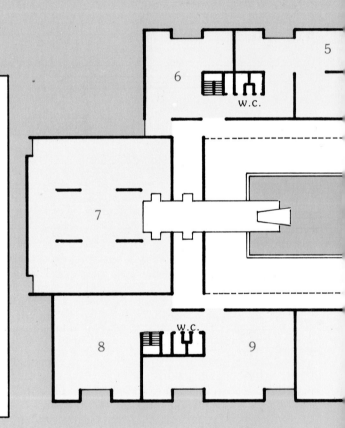

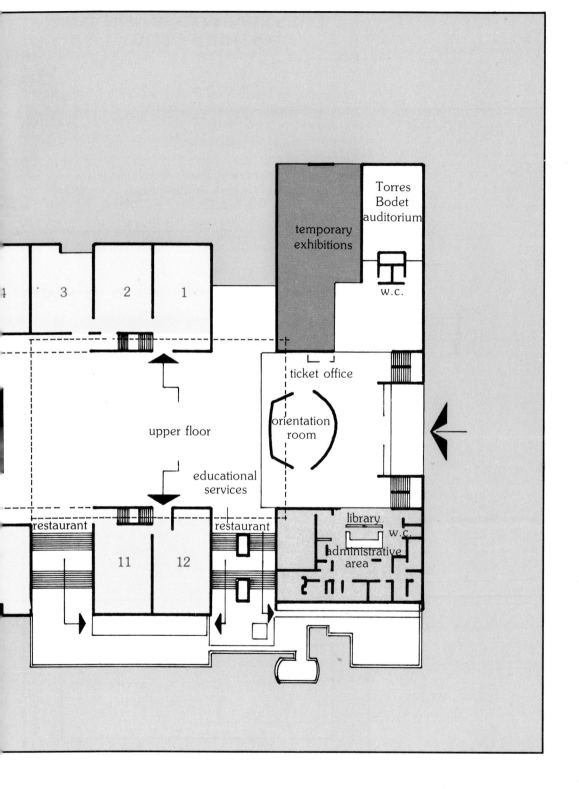

HALL I. INTRODUCTION TO ANTHROPOLOGY

Anthropology is a science which involves the study of man in its widest sense, since it combines in one subject matter, both his biological and social settings. It is the study of man as member of a society and his behaviour within the animal kingdom.

Anthropology is divided into two basic sections: Physical Anthropology and Cultural Anthropology. The first studies the biological aspect of man; his evolution in time and his environmental adaptation. The second studies his behaviour and his cultural development. By culture, we refer to the normal way of life of a group of humans at one particular

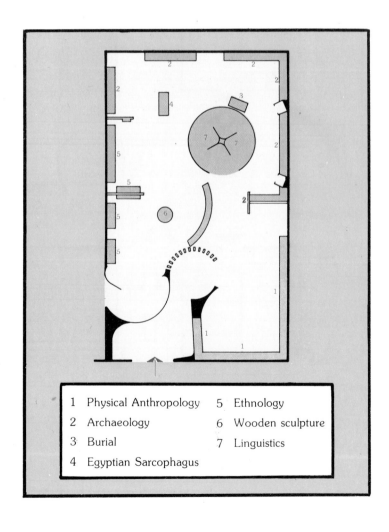

1	Physical Anthropology	5	Ethnology
2	Archaeology	6	Wooden sculpture
3	Burial	7	Linguistics
4	Egyptian Sarcophagus		

time, when they are united in a community with common activities such as hunting, religious or magical practices and defense mechanisms against other groups.

The following sciences are to be found within the Cultural Anthropology field:

Mural painted by Jorge González Camarena, inspired by the different features of women, from various races.

a) Archaeology, which studies and analyze material remains left by man, which help to reconstruct the way of life and the society of the past.
b) Linguistics, which is the study of language; its origins, structure and development through the ages. By a comparative method, it tries to reconstruct the history of language.
c) Ethnology involves the study of the similarities and differences between various human cultures, whether in present day societies or those of the past.

Anthropology, as a science, began at the start of the 19th century, but the fact is that it has its roots in ancient times, when man began to wonder who he was, where he came from and what comes after death; given facts which he still faces, day in and day out.

The ancient Greeks manifested their concern with the subject in the writings of the great historian of the period, Herodo-

Figures showing the *different heights and builds* found within the human race.

tus. It was he who described customs of other nations such as Egypt.

Later, with the discovery of America, mediaeval man's curiosity was aroused to question about himself and his world, when faced with other, up to then, unknown races with an advanced culture.

Father Bernardino of Sahagún is considered the first ethnographer of America, since he wrote detailed descriptions of the Mexica's customs and thus contributed to Anthropology.

A further advance in the field was Charles Darwin's publication of the Theory of Evolution, in which his proposals referred to the biological aspect of man. His theory was that life began from the simplest organisms and evolved into the most complex living organisms, such as in the case of human development, which through millions of years adapted to its environment.

Prehistory is a branch of Anthropology which is the study of the first men to walk the earth, and the traces that they left behind.

Man, as we know him today, developed from an ancestral series of anthropoids. The principal characteristics of the *Homo Sapiens* which differentiate him from the other anthropoids are: he has an erect position, moves on two feet, he has a long period of growth, his lower limbs are longer than the upper limbs, jaw does not project a great deal, he has a parabolic shaped dental arch with much smaller canine teeth and the lack of diastema in the jawbone. He has a prominent nose and lips turned outwards. He has a well defined chin and his brain is twice the size of the anthropoids. The big toe is at the same angle as the rest of the toes. The iliac cavities face forwards instead of inwards. He has little corporal hair and no tactile whiskers and his vision is stereoscopic.

Judging by the results obtained by various methods of the fossils found, we can say that human evolution began with a group of inferior primates represented by "Lemur", who is thought to be some 50 million years old.

The following step in the evolutionary pattern corresponds to a group known as the Propliopitecus who appeared some 35 million years ago. Then came creatures similar to the *Ramapithecus* who existed 14 million years ago. About one and a half million years ago, *Homo Erectus* appeared and may have been related some of the *Australopithecus* species. *Homo Erectus* was able to make tools, hunt larger animals and use fire. This last species covered the entire ancient world, unlike the previous species, whose fossils had only been found in the south and west of the African continent.

Diorama showing a hunting-party in the Lower Paleolithic Age (Europe).

Following these, *Neanderthal Homo Sapiens* appeared about 100 thousand years ago and whose remains were found dispersed throughout a large area which included Europe, North Africa and the Near East. At the end of 50 thousand years of existence, he seems to have disappeared. What happened to *Neanderthal man?* Why have no other remains been found of him after this date? Was he exterminated by *Cro Magnon* man and pushed aside, or did he mix with this later species?

We still have not solved the problem, but what is true, is that we have not found any more fossils. It is probable that he was pushed aside to more inhospitable areas. However, *Homo Sapiens Sapiens,* a human similar to modern man, emerged about 40 thousand years ago.

According to available information, the American man arrived on this continent from Eastern Asia about 30 thousand years ago. During tha glacial period (age), hordes of hunters following the enormous animals (Mammoths), sporadically crossed the land bridges which joined the Asian and American continents by what is known as the Bering Strait.

There is evidence of this prehistoric man in America, in such places as Tepexpan, forty kilometers from Mexico city.

Here the remains, probably of a female, were found under a mound of crusty lime from a warm, dry period, since it was found intact, thus guaranteeing the dating of the find in pleistocenic times. Fossil roots found in the immediate surroundings of the skeleton permitted a dating of about 11 thousand years ago.

Another skull was found in Tlapacoya in the State of Mexico, which is thought to be some nine thousand years old. Given the fact that our most remote ancestors used whatever stick, stone or bone at hand for defense weapons, from the archaeological point of view, it is impossible to detect at which stage these objects were gradually modified. Very slowly the first weapons and tools began to appear when we find tooled stones and bones.

The manufacture of tools and the premeditated modification of raw material was an important step in the process of humanization, therefore the first worked stones are considered to be proof of the appearance of Man.

One of the first archaeological or cultural classifications of prehistoric times, starting from the most recent times to ancient times, is based on the type of implements found. It may be briefly summarized and characterized in the following manner:

Metal Age (copper, bronze, iron): The use of metals overtook fairly rapidly the previous lithic period.
Neolithic Age: Polished stone implements were used together with ceramics, animal domestication and agriculture.

Mesolithic Age: This was the short transitory period between Paleolithic and Neolithic.

Paleolithic Age: A period when worked unpolished stone was used, which can be roughly divided into three sections:

Upper Paleolithic Age - demonstrated the great importance in the use of bone, specialized stone weapons and implements, many homes and burials and considerable development of art as manifested in carvings, sculptures and paintings.

Middle Paleolithic Age -when art was not known but burials appeared and the beginnings of various lithic techniques, including the use of bone artefacts.

Lower Paleolithic Age - Barely specialized lithic artefacts but probable use of fire.

Paleolithic Industries-The first artistic manifestations of a magic/religious nature, as revealed in the cave paintings in the rocky temporary shelters such as the fine examples in Lascaux. Abbot Breuil has referred to it as the prehistoric"Sistine Chapel."Here is great pictoric art, drawn and colored by men of that time, who show us on the walls, superbly stylized bisons, mammoths, bulls, horses and figures full of movement. There are other beautiful paintings in the Altamira cave, near Santander in Spain.

Data on the climate and fauna of the period, archaeological finds and the great pictoric art are the only manifestations available for us to imagine the type of life these men led, who were, in the evolutionary sense, decidedly modern. The so-called *Cro Magnon* species arrived to occupy an extensive area from the Pyrenees to the Dead Sea, judging by the dispersed area of finds of the"Venus" type figurines representing fertility. The figurines show bulky thighs, hips and breasts.

The appearance of agriculture was a great step in the cultural evolution of man. It made him less susceptible to the vicissitudes of nature, and thus he could have a permanent dwelling and could form small hamlets. With time, land produced extra food, silos were built and they began to store grain. This produced a greater amount of collective security, which in turn, allowed certain members of the community time for more specialized work and so the artisans appeared, which made commerce possible.

•Funerary practises existed from the most remote times. Sedentary life began slowly with first a group of dwellings converting into hamlets. This gave rise to cementeries or collective tombs where numerous buried skeletons have been found. The two most frequent forms of burial were, either in an extended position, or flexed, with the knees doubled up under the chin. There also existed the cremation rite for the bodies, possibly in awe of the dead who were rendered all sorts of honors.

Burial customs evolved into the building of special tombs for the great lords, or high priests both in the Old World, such as in Egypt and in the New World, as in Palenque.

It is difficult to believe that agriculture was invented only once in the history of humanity. Plants cultivated in Prehispanic America and the Old World were of different botanical species. Furthermore, the cereal agriculture of Europe and the Middle East is markedly different from the horticulture practiced in Southeast Asia. These are fundamental differences and suggest, at least, three different origins and three different times for the invention of agriculture.

The invention of pottery, to be able to make vessels of mud mixed with water and fired, must also have been the result of many trials. It shows the necessity to start looking for suitable clay deposits which contained aluminum silicate. Then the material had to be mixed with a certain quantity of water to form a paste that would be maleable. Later they had to add a substance to remove the grease which might be fine sand, shell or pulverized stone which would distribute the tensions created within the mud when fired to prevent it from cracking. The process continued taking shape. Whilst the smaller objects were moulded directly, the larger objects had to be made of long strips of clay which were rolled round in a special form until the desired shape was obtained. The joint would then be pressed out. It was much later when the potter's wheel was invented, that the final stage was reached and the surface was decorated with regular impres-

Example of a North American Indian dwelling.

24

Reproduction of the *Egyptian god Tot* who governed writing and the sciences.

sions, incisions or pinches. After that, the piece would be left to dry in the shade and then in the sun and decorated with colors and figures.

Finally the firing, which was when the piece was subjected to a temperature of nearly 600°C, not an easy feat in open air. This had to be achieved by partially covering the fire which would make a kind of oven.

Even when the vessels are fragile, the remains are remarkably indestructible. The sherds are unharmed by contact with the earth and humidity and, as these fragments had no particular value, they very often remain in the place they were originally thrown and have remained there for centuries. These garbage dumps are wonderful sources of information for the archeologist. The successive order of layers in which they are found on excavation and the variations in the type of earthenware decorative styles, provide a strata column which reflects the permanency or cultural changes of the ancient inhabitants of the place.

These early inventions of man gave rise to others, such as the wheel in the Old World, harnessing of animals, the making of bread, cheese, alcoholic fermentation, the cooking of food, spinning and weaving, dress, building, carpentry refinements and mining. Together with these, deve-

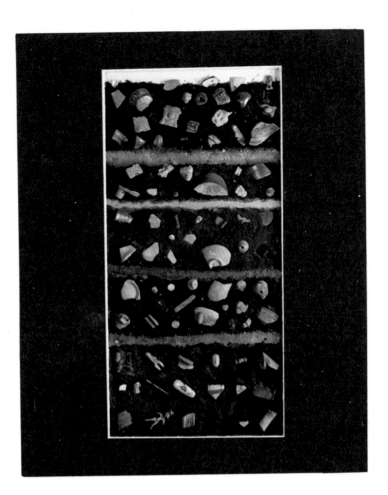

Stratified layers show human occupation. Reconstruction of geological-cultural section of the Valley of Mexico showing the changes of objects and pottery through the different periods of time.

loped irrigation, commerce, sea and land transport, political and social organization and the invention of writing.

The human groups in Mesoamerica developed their inventions in various spheres such as agriculture. They invented the "chinampa" a floating piece of artificial land to plant, the planting stick, cultivation of "chia", a seed to extract oil and a kind of drink, cultivation of maguey for pulque or to make paper, cultivation of cocoa, grinding of the maize cooked with lime or ash, ritual use of paper and rubber, religious festivals, religious calendar of 260 days and the solar calendar of 365 days, hieroglyphic writing, códices, stepped pyramids and great development in the arts and organized commerce.

HALL 2. MESOAMERICA

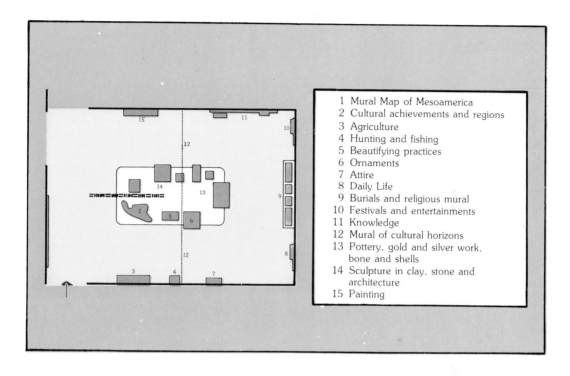

1 Mural Map of Mesoamerica
2 Cultural achievements and regions
3 Agriculture
4 Hunting and fishing
5 Beautifying practices
6 Ornaments
7 Attire
8 Daily Life
9 Burials and religious mural
10 Festivals and entertainments
11 Knowledge
12 Mural of cultural horizons
13 Pottery, gold and silver work, bone and shells
14 Sculpture in clay, stone and architecture
15 Painting

MESOAMERICA: CULTURAL CONCEPT

The term Mesoamerica is not a geographical concept, but designates an area with a series of cultural features common to the different groups who settled there, even though there are various regional differences. In general terms, one can say that the high cultural level achieved in Mesoamerica followed parallel lines and culminated in proper civilizations in some cases.

The Mesoamerican region stretches from the Río Soto la Marina in Tamaulipas in the north, as far as the Río Sinaloa in the West of Mexico. The southern limits reach the Gulf of Nicoya in Costa Rica and Río Motagua in Honduras. Nevertheless, there are fixed boundaries, particularly in the northern area which changed considerably with time due to expansion or the opposite, according to the various periods of flourishing or weakness through which it passed.

This map shows the area which is defined as Mesoamerica. It shows the general boundaries and the most characteristic features of the principal prehispanic cultures.

Towards the west, we can see the Guasave, Chametla and Sinaloa pottery, the hollow figurines and dogs of Coli-

ma, the Mezcala type of stone work, characteristic of Guerrero and the Yácatas and the pipes of Michoacán. In the south, in the Oaxaca region, we see Zapotecan urns and a carved stone. Metal work and the polychrome Mixtecan ceramics, are also represented here.

To the west, the Huaxtecans are represented by their ceramics and sculpture; Veracruz by "palms", "axes" and smiling faces, and the Olmecs by the colossal heads.

The central area shows the monumental sculpture of Tula, a twin Mexican temple, the Xochicalco stele, Teotihuacán ceramics painted al fresco and the multicolored Cholula pottery.

In the south, we find an example of the typical Mayan architecture, stone work and ceramics.

We have divided the Mesoamerican territory into five large cultural regions, West Mexico, Central Plateau, Gulf Coast, Oaxaca, Mayan Area. Various cultures developed in these regions during the passage of time, so we have divided them into three main historical-cultural periods.

EVOLUTION AND DEVELOPMENT OF THE MESOAMERICAN CULTURES

Dogs, rabbits, fish and crabs formed part of man's diet.

Preclassic (1800-100 BC)

The original groups of inhabitants who had hunted and gathered, became farmers and began a sedentary existence in small hamlets. Pottery changed from rough, single colored work in the first stages, to two colored and polychromed, with more varied and complicated shapes. The first figurines, which were mainly female and clumsy, slowly developed until an excellent quality was produced, since now, the priest class emerged, the cult to tohe gods, burial sites and the first construction of the pyramid bases began. At the same time amongst some of the group, the beginnings of an hieroglyphic writing emerged.

Classic (100 BC - 900 AC)

This was the period when the great cultures flourished and the ceremonial centers were built, forming proper cities that not only contained the buildings dedicated to the religious cults, but also where the administrative centers were

found with the noblemen's residences, the workshops, etcetera.

Ceramics and figurines were produced in a wide range of shapes and with different production techniques. At the same time, there was a boom in the arts (architecture, sculpture and painting). Scientific knowledge also increased and with it came further advances, mainly in astronomy and mathematics. More complicated writing developed amongst some groups and religion became a basic focal point from which a theocratic government developed.

Postclassic (900 - 1521 A.D.)

As time passed, the theocratic society converted into a militaristic one and leaders emerged, warring against the neighboring communities. The conquered nations were subjected and paid tribute to others. In this militant atmosphere, fortified cities emerged.

Metalurgy and artificial irrigation were introduced, and the codices show how much writing developed, to such an extent, that some groups such as the Mayas and Mexicas, employed indeaographic and phonetic characters.

What is also true, is that in some regions, there were signs of decadence, such as in the center where the Mexicas dominated large territories and were trying to strengthen their new empire which eventually ended violently with the Spanish Conquest.

Male figurine made of lozenge shaped clay.

Smiling face.

AGRICULTURE

Some of the personal ornaments used in the Mesoamerican cultures: *ear plug. underlip plug. pendant and necklace.*

The Mesoamerican communities were principally farmers cultivating their main crops of maize, beans, squash and chile which were the basis of their diet.

Some communities used marsh land or flooding systems for cultivation, planting on the edge of lakes and rivers. Others in the valleys and slopes used a slash and burn system and yet others, divised a terracing system that provided a greater surface area.At a later period, artificial irrigation was devised by a system of canals and the use of "chinampas" (artificial islands of fertile land) and gardens.

Both men and women were employed in agricultural activities and the implements used, such as planting sticks, axes, hoes or spades, were made of stone or wood. With the introduction of metals, some implements were made of copper in some regions.

Apart from the crops mentioned, a great number of edible plants and medicinal plants were cultivated. With the Span-

31

Urn burial.

ish Conquest many of these plants were introduced into the western world. Among the Mesoamerican contributions are included the avocado, the sapota, amaranth, cocoa, etc.

The Mesoamerican settlers complemented their diet with hunting animals such as deer, turkey, wild boar, duck, rabbit, partridge, turtle, crab, sea snail, fish, clams, etc. Furthermore, they collected honey, insect larvae, fruit, roots, tuber, etc. which varied in different regions.

For these activities they used a variety of weapons and artefacts which included the *átlatl* or blow gun, bows and arrows, lances, slings, traps, nets, fishhooks, stockades and even poison.

CLOTHING

The Mesoamerican peoples generally used simple clothing, basically differenciated by the quality of materials and ornamentation according to social rank. The men normally wore a *máxtlatl*, or a kind of loin cloth and a cape, the women, an underskirt or skirt and a *huipil*, or blouse.

CUSTOMS AND ADORNMENTS

Some groups considered the deformation of the skull an embellishment, others mutilated the teeth, painted the body, tatooed themselves, scarred themselves, purposely induced cross-eyes, perforated the earlobes, the nasal septum or under the lower lip to use ear, nose, and lip plugs.

Apart from the customs mentioned above, the Mesoamericans also adorned themselves with a great variety of ornaments; necklaces, rings, pectorals, pendants and bracelets made of a variety of raw material such as obsidian, rock crystal, bone, shell, jadeite, gold, silver, copper and turquoise.

Scale model of the *Great Temple* of Mexico-Tenochtitlan.

These objects are not only impressive for their beauty, but also for their delicate and exquisite workmanship.

SOCIAL STRATA

Generally speaking, we can say that the Mesoamerican societies were divided into social classes: a privileged elite, made up of noblemen, high priests and military chiefs; an intermediary class composed of warriors, lower ranking priests, merchants and specialized craftsmen and the working class, which was the majority of the population including farmers and small time craftsmen, who basically sustained the upper and middle class.

RELIGION

There was a polytheistic religion and although the names of the gods changed according to the region, its basic characteristics were similar. Thus we see the predominant god of rain appears throughout Mesoamerica with various names such as Tláloc, Cocijo, Tajín, Chaac, Chupi-Tirípeme.

Human sacrifice was one of the many rituals practiced throughout Mesoamerica. It was not the cruel practice that the Spaniards qualified it, but another way in which to appease the gods and thus preserve the balance of the universe.

In view of the fact that religion was such an important aspect, death also played a role of prime importance. Some of the different burial methods practised are shown in this hall, mainly buried in urns sideways, in front or back position, either individually or collectively.

CULTURE

Among the most important achievements reached by the Mesoamerican peoples was a vigesimal positional numerical system, which implied an understanding of the use of the zero, the development of a calendar based on astronomic observations, a wide knowledge of medicine, the capacity to produce codices, a very highly developed architecture, etc. There was also an enormous development in craftmanship, of arts ranging from metalurgy, ceramics, bone and shell carving, earthenware sculpture, stone carving, painting and tomb construction.

The hall concludes by showing the visitor the architectonic development of the varying temple pyramidal bases constructed in Mesoamerica, from the simplest example in Tepalcate Hill, to the Great Temple of Tenochtitlan.

HALL 3. ORIGINS

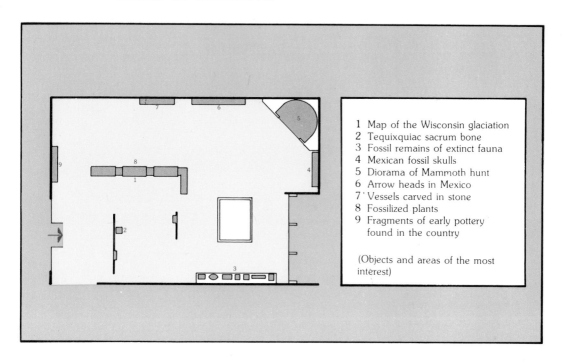

1 Map of the Wisconsin glaciation
2 Tequixquiac sacrum bone
3 Fossil remains of extinct fauna
4 Mexican fossil skulls
5 Diorama of Mammoth hunt
6 Arrow heads in Mexico
7 Vessels carved in stone
8 Fossilized plants
9 Fragments of early pottery
found in the country

(Objects and areas of the most interest)

THE FIRST SETTLERS

About three million years ago, the earth suffered a series of glaciations, sheets of ice and snow which, in some cases, were thousands of yards thick, covering part of the continents and causing the natural level of the sea fo fall. During these first three million years there were greater, or lesser glacier advances, with intervals of warm and hot climatic conditions. In these lapses, the glaciers retreated and remained in the polar region and mountain tops.

The first settlers in America came across the Bering Strait in the last glacial period, called Wisconsin in America, and Würm, in Europe. The Bering Strait is only 40 meters deep and, as the waters of the sea had decreased by some 50 meters on several occasions, this stretch was passable where the continents joined. There were times when the sea went down to its lowest level between 100 and 110 meters and revealed an earth mass that was given the name of Beringia.

With this in mind, it is easy to imagine crossing by foot during the greatest glacial period Wisconsin, which began some 60,000 years ago and ended approximately 18,000 years ago. During the three glacial periods that were mentioned previously, no species related to man had set foot

in America. The nomads who ventured into our continent were the Homo Sapiens belonging to the Mongoloid group. About 6,000 B.C. the pass was definitely closed and the present day configuration of the region was established. However, we do not discard the idea that there were other later transoceanic contacts, particularly with small groups of Australoids and Melanesoids.

DIORAMA: MAMMOTH HUNT

The lakey districts of our country preserved the fossil remains of fauna and mammoths, amongst other species, which enable us to reproduce archaeologically, the probable way of life of the men who inhabited it approximately 12,000 years ago.

The importance of these finds rests in the archaeological association of the various artefacts, such as the points of projectiles, rakes, scrapers and knives. All of them were carved of stone and used to kill, and cut up animals, clearly demonstrating the presence of man at this period.

The Tepexpan - Iztapan area is reproduced here to show the type of hunting that must have taken place in other lacustrine regions in the country, since a considerable number of bone remnants have been found to testify such activity.

The large animals, when going to water in the great lakes, were trapped in the muddy bottom. Prehistoric man took

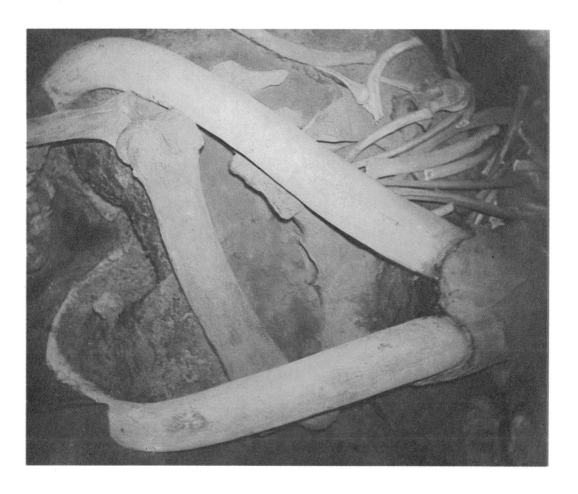

advantage of the situation to pursue them, which would have been the only way that the rudimentary weapons available would have permitted them to hunt these enormous animals. The meat obtained complemented their basic diet of fruit, seed and wild vegetable gathering, and their skins would serve to make simple garments and shelter for their dwellings.

Reconstruction of the excavation of *Mammoth No. 2* found in Santa Isabel Iztapan in the State of Mexico.

MODEL OF THE VALLEY OF MEXICO

Our ancient great lake had fluvial origins and was formed during the pleistocenic age. Important finds of animal, and human bones have been located at its edges, including many prehistoric artefacts.

During the nineteenth century this extensive lake was known by several names, depending on the villages situated on its banks, so that in parts, it was known as the Lake of Texcoco, Lake of Mexico Xaltocan, Zumpango and Chalco-

Xochimilco. The latter, had fresh water, unlike Texcoco in the north, which was larger and contained salt water, except in its northern extreme which was freshwater.

Climatic temperature changes, rainy season changes, diminishing volume of water into the subsoil, were the natural causes for the level of the lake to lower, causing certain portions of earth to appear, forming islands and peninsulas which were previously under water.

The aztecs were the first to drain part of the lake to establish their city. The situation grew worse as the settlements grew and it became more and more necessary for men to intervene in altering the lake's physionomy.

PREHISTORY IN MEXICO

The use of stone implements was basic to the economy of the prehistoric groups. It is through them, that we are able to understand their cultures. We have seen that they manufactured implements such as rakes, scrapers, slicers, knives and spearheads. These groups depended on a gathering economy expressed in hunting. However, we notice that they also had grinding stones, pestels and mortars which showed that they had a combination economy of gathering to compliment their diet. Stone served for a number of uses, to obtain food, for defense, for building or as an implement to manufacture other artefacts.

Prehistory in Mexico has been divided into three large sections.

Arrow heads of different shapes and sizes, used by hunters of the Cenolithic period in Mexico. One shows the possible way in which they were attached to a shaft.

Archeolithic (Ancient Stone Age)

This period was roughly between 60,000 and 12,000 BC on the American continent and in Mexico in particular, was between 30,000 and 12,000 BC.

Cenolithic (Recent Stone Age)

This period is divided into two phases according to the progress of each culture. The lower phase was between 12,000 and 7,000 BC. The men of this period were still hunters and gatherers unlike the upper period between 7,000 and 5,000 BC who made the first steps towards domestication.

Proto neolithic

This was a transition period 5,000 - 2,000 BC in which the first settlements, hamlets and pottery appeared among semi-sedentary groups.

Group of objects made of natural fibres: ropes, net, sandals, fragment of rush matting, fragment of cotton.

Throughout the first period the generic organizations were nomadic groups-food gatherers, whose social structure was based on the family nucleus. It was probably during the Cenolithic period when groups of about 30 individuals collected together in hunting bands, since cooperation was essential for the success of an activity in which weapons were still very rudimentary. Already in the Lower Cenolithic period, the first spear heads had been crafted and these techniques were improved to make other artefacts that would be useful for the hunt. Archaeological research indicates that since 12,000 BC, hunting was an activity of groups of people who were essentially gatherers of fruit, seeds and wild vegetables and it served to supplement this basic diet and provide them with skins for garments and perhaps rudimentary shelters.

These early inhabitants frequently hunted smaller animals such as lizards, iguanas, snakes, etc. also various bird species situated in the lake regions of Mexico. At the same time, they also collected eggs, of both birds and other animals such as ants.

We know that during the Cenolithic period, stone working techniques improved by polishing and burnishing to acquire better finish. Bones were used to achieve this and were also used to divise other implements and for even artistic purposes. The Tequixquiac Clanc Sacro fossil is an example of a beautiful piece of work, the only example of prehistoric household art found in Mexico, and has been dated around 12,000 BC.

Sites corresponding to these periods are, to name a few, Santa Isabel Iztapan in the state of Mexico, El Riego Caves, Texcal and Coxcatlan in the state of Puebla, Devil's Cave in Tamaulipas and El Cedral, in San Luis Potosí.

The last prehistoric period in Mexico, the Protoneolithic, is a transition period in which gathering, hunting and fishing continued and apart from the cultivation of plants which began around 3,000 BC, small settlements began to appear with partially underground houses. The inhabitants were still semi-sedentary and subject to having to wait for harvesting of the crops planted. Soon, however, they began to make simple earthenware vessels and pottery began to appear around 2,300 BC. They began to polish stone and to domesticate dogs. As a consequence of increased vegetable cultivation in greater quantities, sedentary conditions accelerated. This was how, between 2,300 and 2,000 BC, the first farming communities emerged in the enormous cultural area which we call Mesoamerica. This has been named the Preclassic or Formative period and marks the beginning of the ancient or prehispanic history of Mexico.

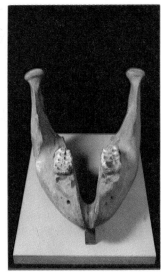

Coast Settlements

During the cenolithic period, man began to explore the resources of the sea, particularly on the Pacific coast, proved by the mounds of sea shells called "concheros" (shell middens). While these mounds were being explored the remains of animals, hearth residues and stone artefacts were found. The oldest "conchero" found in the region of San Blas, Nayarit dates between 3,000 and 1,000 BC. The oldest cultural complexes studied in this region are known as "Matachen" and "San Blas", covering a period between the third and fifth milenium BC.

Plant Domestication

Evidence of man's interest in the plants that could be used to extract sugar, such as "mesquite" prickly pear and "maguey" cactus is so remote that it is difficult to pinpoint the date. However, about 7,000 BC vegetable species began to be cultivated, such as various types of squash, avocados, sapota, chiles, beans, cotton and later maize. This created a better diet and a greater freedom from the surroundings. It showed a great cultural step forward, placing man in the position of producing food. As the agricultural products improved, others developed and as a consequence, the groups were well on the way to a definitely sedentary existence with accompanying cultural advances.

Left. Fossilized sacrum of camel like quadruped with the appearance of a canine head. Bone found in Tequixquiac. State of Mexico.

Rigth.
Fossil of the *jawbone of a Mastodon.*

41

Various *lithic objects*.

The earliest evidence of this phase which occurred in Mexico, has been found in Caves and Sites in Chihuahua, Durango, Coahuila, Hidalgo, San Blas and Matachen in Nayarit, in the Southwest and Caves in the Tamaulipas Sierra, the Zoaphilco Cave in Mexico, Yanhuitlán in Oaxaca, Santa Martha Cave in Chiapas, and Tehuacán, Puebla.

POTTERY BEGINNINGS

Pottery first appeared when man became more sedentary. It was first moulded by hand in globular shapes of badly baked mud. The oldest examples of vessels with very simple decoration dating from 1,500 BC were found in Tehuacán, Puebla. These correspond to a phase denominated "Ajalpan" and a similar dating has been put to other pottery found in Colima, El Opeño in Michoacán, Chiapa de Corzo and Tierras Largas in Oaxaca. In the state of Guerrero and Chiapas three other types of pottery were found and called "Pox" in Puerto Marquez, Acapulco, dated about 2,300 BC. "Barra" and "Ocós" on the coast of Chiapas related to Central and South America with a date around 2,000 BC. Furthermore, the "Flacco" and "Almagre" of Tamaulipas and the "Zoaphilco" in central Mexico correspond to a similar dating.

Only sherds remain of these vessels, from which, we have tried to derive their original use and the way in which they were made.

When man became sedentary and began to produce food, he developed a cultural evolution that brought with it significant advances and new inventions, such as commerce, religion and the calendar, among many other things.

This important step began in Mexico within the simple settlements situated near the rivers, lakes and springs which allowed the survival of man himself and his crops. To begin with, the first dwellings were partially underground shelters which were built of perishable materials and therefore difficult to preserve. However, a settlement of this type has been explored in Chilac in the state of Puebla and dates from about 3,000 BC.

Only a few sherds remain of the *pottery* of this period. This is a possible reconstruction.

HALL 4. PRECLASSIC

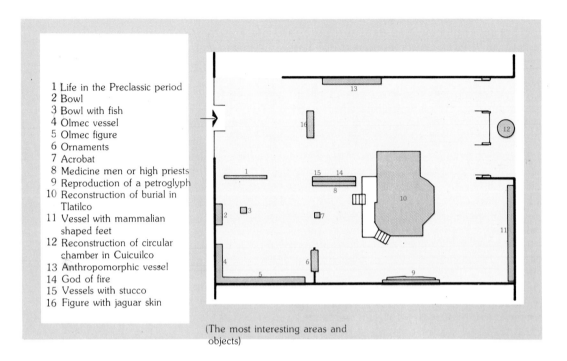

1 Life in the Preclassic period
2 Bowl
3 Bowl with fish
4 Olmec vessel
5 Olmec figure
6 Ornaments
7 Acrobat
8 Medicine men or high priests
9 Reproduction of a petroglyph
10 Reconstruction of burial in Tlatilco
11 Vessel with mammalian shaped feet
12 Reconstruction of circular chamber in Cuicuilco
13 Anthropomorphic vessel
14 God of fire
15 Vessels with stucco
16 Figure with jaguar skin

(The most interesting areas and objects)

PRECLASSIC PERIOD IN THE CENTRAL PLATEAU

ORIGINS OF MESOAMERICAN CULTURES

The prehispanic inhabitants of Mexico all had a traditional culture from a common origin which, through time, evolved varying degrees of progress.

When the hunting-gathering groups settled in one place, converting into a sedentary society, they began a long process of technological, economic and social achievements. This change marked the beginning of the Preclassic of Formative period, whose principal characteristics were agriculture and pottery. This was the basis of what would later be the Mesoamerican culture.

The period was divided in three phases: Lower Preclassic (1800-1300 BC), Middle Preclassic, (1300 - 800 BC) and Upper Preclassic (800 BC - 100 AD) each one having their particular characteristics that differentiate them from the others.

ECONOMY

These settlers had a self sufficient economy which was mainly based on the farming of maize, beans, amaranth (nowadays widely sold as candy known as "alegría" —joy—), etc., and complemented with hunting, fishing and harvesting.

AGRICULTURE

Initially, agricultural systems must have been very simple, cultivating the lower regions that would have been periodically flooded by the water of lakes and rivers and the seasonal rains. A planting stick, tillers, stone axes and possibly wooden hoes were used to plant seeds.

THE FIRST CENTERS

At the end of this period, the first ceremonial centers were built, showing tremendous progress and complexity, both in the social, and economic organization.

It is possible that the division of work and social classes occurred at this time. They were probably divided according to their activities, for example, farmers, hunters, potters, stonemasons, basket weavers and tanners.

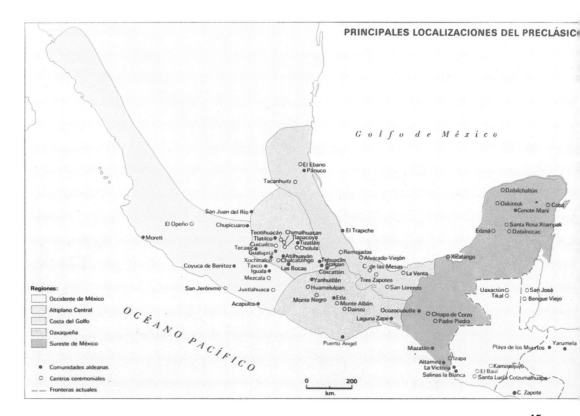

PRINCIPALES LOCALIZACIONES DEL PRECLÁSICO

Upper Preclassic *vessels* with
geometric incisions, found in
Tlatilco, State of Mexico.

SOCIAL ORGANIZATION

Social organization was based orginally on the family and
their relatives. Little by little, certain people who had gained
prestige among the community began to rule the group and
conduct the magic-religious practices of what was then a
simple cult. These people have been identified as priests
or "chamanes".

The Preclassic era formed the elements which were later
to chrystalize into the Classic Mesoamerican period whose
maximum expression was found on the Central Plateau in
Teotihuacán.

EARLY PRECLASSIC PERIOD

During the Early Preclassic period, monochromed pottery was elaborated, that is one single color, either black,
brown, red or white in a great variety of shapes: bottles,

plates, "pulque" bowls and pots, either for every day use, or as burial offerings.

Decoration consisted in geometric designs made of fine incisions. Furthermore, they made clay female figurines that were probably related to fertility

The ceramic traditions continued their development until during the Middle Preclassic period, two types of vessels were produced combining red and brown for example, at the same time that the monochromed vessels were being produced. Some of the bottoms of these items were decorated with different motifs, such as natural elements like animals, fruits, plants and stars.

MIDDLE PRECLASSIC

Approximately towards the year 1,200 BC, the Olmec group coming from the Gulf of Mexico left traces of their ideas and customs throughout a vast area of ancient Mexico.

Clay masks used by the high priests, from Tlatilco, State of Mexico.

Left.
Upper Preclassic clay
representation of the *God of Fire*,
from Cuicuilco, Federal District.

Right.
Two-colored *clay vessel*
representing a human head.

Their presence was manifested in pottery manufactured in the Central Plateau, with their particular characteristics of thick sides and "flat bottoms". They were predominately made of one color, either black or white with smoked parts. They were mainly decorated in motifs related to the jaguar, which were incised and then rubbed with red powder.

The Olmecs enriched the local ideas in all aspects. They imbued pottery with a great variety of anthropomorphic, phytomorphic or zoomorphic figures or a combination of all of them. The "pulque bowls" are kidney shaped and the plates have a lip.

The local figurines mixed with the Olmec style, resulting in others with bulbous legs, shaved heads, plump faces, etc.

Physical adornment was of particular importance amongst the village groups and this is reflected in the figurines with faces and bodies painted in white, red and yellow colors, sometimes with geometric designs.

They did not rely on ear plugs, necklaces, lip plugs bracelets, pectorals or throttlers to compliment the corporal painting but the hairdressing was very elaborate, in a kind of tur-

ban. Some of the figurines show various types of garments such as underskirts, waistcoats, jackets, trousers, hats, etc.

With time, religious ideas became more complex and in the Middle Preclassic period, earthenware representations of high priests emerged. These dignitaries are shown wearing varying headdresses and caps and even masks. These figurines show an important transition since the new deities were now personified and transmitted their desires through the human element.

The inhabitants of the Valley of Mexico enjoyed a rich natural environment both in flora and fauna. There were numerous pine, evergreen, oak and sandalwood forests,

49

cypress in the lower parts, tulle trees at the edge of the lake. Animals such as deer, armadillo, "zirigüe", "tlacuache", a great variety of migrating birds, frogs, toads, white fish, etc. flourished in this environment and served as food.

Some of these animals were represented in earthenware figures and add to our knowledge of the environment in which these peoples lived at the time.

UPPER CLASSIC

A flow of new ideas reached the Central Plateau in the Upper Preclassic period, from Chupícuaro, Guanajuato in the west of Mexico. Some of these cultural influences were assimilated and were reflected in the pottery, such as the conical, high mammiform supports with borders near the base; in the grooved vessels with "al fresco" decoration and in the use of the negative technique.

One of the techniques used in vessel decoration in the West of Mexico was to model parts of the human figure and complete it with paint. This technique was used in various examples of the later Upper Preclassic period. At the same time, small conical shaped globs of mud were aplied as supports called "buttons". These elements reached their zenith during the Classic period of Teotihuacán.

The manufacturing techniques from the West of Mexico were well received in the Central Plateau and were immediately applied locally, imitating the shapes, since the use of polychrome was only employed in painting "al fresco". The finish of the vessels was achieved by using red on buff, as is demonstrated in the pottery found in the Ticomán site.

One of the earliest representations of the old God of Fire was found in Cuicuilco, Federal District. This is probably the place where the cult to fire began.

Cuicuilco is among the first centers where pyramid temple bases were constructed, together with others in Tlapacoya, Tepalcate Hill and Teotihuacán. Cuicuilco is particularly impressive for its size. This growing ceremonial center was interrupted in its development by a volcanic eruption, the lava of which now forms Pedregal de San Angel.

Various shapes and decorations coming from the West were adopted in the Valley of Mexico. This piece, found in tomb No. 3 in Tlapacoya shows this influence. Well finished vessels of this type were used in burial offerings of important dignitaries such as high priests or governors.

Tlapacoya was among the first temple bases built in the Valley of Mexico.

HALL 5. TEOTIHUACAN

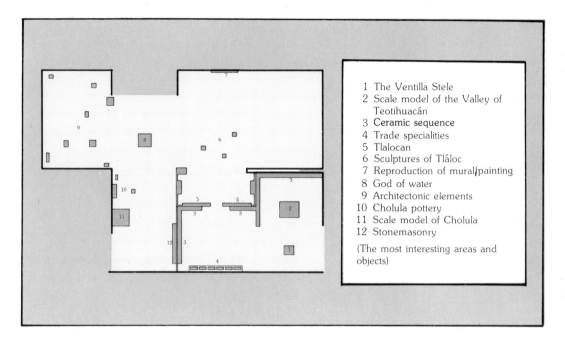

1 The Ventilla Stele
2 Scale model of the Valley of Teotihuacán
3 **Ceramic sequence**
4 Trade specialities
5 Tlalocan
6 Sculptures of Tláloc
7 Reproduction of mural painting
8 God of water
9 Architectonic elements
10 Cholula pottery
11 Scale model of Cholula
12 Stonemasonry

(The most interesting areas and objects)

TEOTIHUACAN: CITY OF THE GODS

After a long process of development, the ancient inhabitants of the Valley of Mexico, transformed their way of life. This new historic period known as the Urban or Classic period, dates between 100 BC and 800 AD and is characterized by the emergence of the great urban center of Teotihuacán. This large city covering 22 km² with its considerable population, was geographically situated in the Valley of Mexico, influencing the entire valley and later the Puebla and Tlaxcala Valleys and Morelos. Through its power over these other regions, the Teotihuacán people established contacts with both the Gulf Coast and the Pacific Coast and even reached as far south as Guatemala and El Salvador.

The economy was basically agricultural but all the economic, political and religious power was centered in this great city of Teotihuacán. Its great power and strength is difficult to understand without considering the existence of a defined social work division. The great building constructions, the abundance of materials and the wide distribution of Teotihuacán objects and pottery throughout Mesoamerican territory, are some of the elements that effectively indicate well established institutions and organizations. These include the production of handcrafts, engineering, organized commerce,

51

This reproduction of *Tlalocan* shows how important maize and beans were in prehispanic life.

established religious cults, etc. which were all characteristics concentrated in converting Teotihuacán into an attractive secular and sacred center known by the communities throughout the land.

There still exist a large number of material manifestations of this society, from the bone remains of individuals and instruments of everyday life, to the graphic representations of religious thought and aesthetic ideals.

In the following pages, we will present some of the most interesting materials that has been collected by people interested in the prehispanic history and is now found in the National Anthropology Museum.

TEOTIHUACAN ARCHITECTURE

It was Teotihuacán that revealed, what is now called, an urban revolution. This new form of life implied problems

which were solved by changes in social relationships. Thus, one of the most typical features in the Classic horizon was the development of an economy concentrated in a great urban center. This center was particularly innovative in its planning through a grid system of different sections and buildings. Public services were organized, such as markets, sanitation and a division of boroughs according to the specific work produced. These urban elements amongst others present in Teotihuacán, permit us to call it a city.

One can distinguish the civil and religious units in Teotihuacán and among the first, we can mention the workshops

Left. Agriculture was complemented with hunting in which arrow heads such as this one, were used.

Right.
Marker for the ball game, known as the Ventilla Stele.

and the living quarters. Among the second, are the temples and altars dedicated to different deities. Both types of buildings were fundamentally constructed of stone and earth with probably the frequent use of wood. Both civil and religious buildings had a stucco finish which was very often painted with the different ideas, particularly religious, of the Teotihuacán people. The majority of these paintings were colored with mineral and plant pigments, particularly red, yellow, green, white and black.

One of the specialities of Teotihuacán was its construction. The monumentality of its buildings and the discovery of some of the implements speaks of very specialized work. It is probable that the man-time factor used in construction was applied.

STONEMASONRY

Teotihuacán achieved a considerable degree of finesse in stonemasonry particularly since, as in all Mesoamerica,

Pot showing a representation of *Tláloc*, from Teotihuacán.

The ancient inhabitants of Teotihuacán also expressed some of their customs and dress in clay. Origin, Teotihuacán.

their work tools both for crafts and agriculture, were made of stone or wood. This fact alone, is evidence of the high degree of social organization which Teotihuacán must have achieved.

We can appreciate the different stages in the work process by seeing the instruments they used to work other materials such as shell, bone, and semiprecious stones, considered luxury items. Since the implements used were of stone it seems that stone-masons achieved a special status. Various rocks that were used included obsidian or volcanic crystal whose properties permitted effective sharp-pointed instruments to be made in a great variety. The importance of this group of laborers has been confirmed by archaeological finds of workshops where obsidian implements were made. It is worthwhile mentioning here, that one of these workshops was found near the Plaza of the Moon which shows how the social importance of this craft which must have been controlled by the highest order of the Teotihuacán society.

The Teotihuacán people also used a variety of stone on which to project their religious and artistic ideas. For example, they were able to impart some of the physical characteristics of the population and express diferent facial features seen in the ancient inhabitants of the city. They also manufactured personal adornments and magnificent objects of stone.

CERAMICS

Individual characteristics of the population were also expressed in ceramic objects. Innumerable figurines have been found in Teotihuacán and it is from these, we have an idea of the garments worn by the ancient inhabitants. We know from these figurines that the women used a kind of under skirt and an overblouse *quechquémitl*, a fashion which has lasted till the present day. Men used, among other garments, loin cloths and headdresses. It is also possible to deduce, that certain adornments and garments were used particularly for special occasions and at certain times.

The majority of vessels made by the Teotihuacán people were earthenware, principally from the clay found in the valley of Teotihuacán itself. However, for other types of pottery such as the "thin orange" type, they used other clay found outside the Valley of Mexico. They used a variety of shapes for the pots, cajetes and other more specific vessels such as "patojos"with a squat shape, amid the innumerable vessels found.

The Teotihuacán craftsman decorated his pots using a number of techniques from smoothing and polishing, to the most varied stucco applications and painted designs. Among the most unusual techniques is the use of "appliqué"; in the bowls, for example, they applied a series of earthenware ribbing which formed images of the god Tláloc.

RELIGION

Religion played an extremely important role in Teotihuacán and reflected both ritual aspects and the different elements of everyday life determined by the fundamental agricultural activity of the Teotihuacán people. In fact, predominant among the remains left by the ancient inhabitants of Teotihuacán, were representations of the god of the rain, Tláloc. The fundamental representations of this deity were processed in a wide variety of materials; there is still preserved, for example, a huge memorial tablet with a stylistic interpretation of the god.

There are few known facts about the rituals practiced in Teotihuacán, but one of them is the famous ball game. Although we have not found the architectonical remains of

the ball court, we do know, through other evidence, that this ritual was practiced in the City of the Gods. One of the proofs of this is the marker known as the Ventilla Stele.

The oldest known deity reverenced in the Valley of Mexico and often found in Teotihuacán, is the Old God of Fire and his cult originates in the Preclassic period.

Around 600 BC the great city of Teotihuacán was abandoned yet many of its social and cultural elements lasted throughout the rich Mesoamerican traditions.

Huehuetéotl, the Old God of Fire, was among the most important of the Teotihuacán deities.

HALL 6. THE TOLTECS

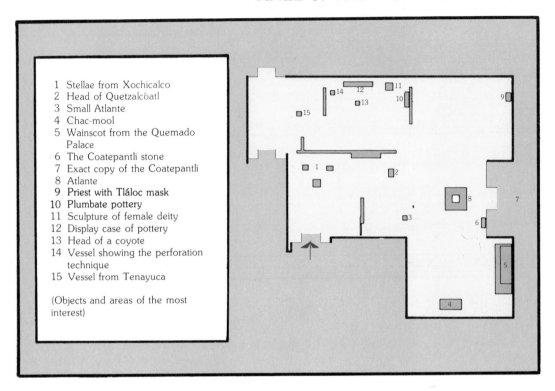

1 Stellae from Xochicalco
2 Head of Quetzalcóatl
3 Small Atlante
4 Chac-mool
5 Wainscot from the Quemado
   Palace
6 The Coatepantli stone
7 Exact copy of the Coatepantli
8 Atlante
9 Priest with Tláloc mask
10 Plumbate pottery
11 Sculpture of female deity
12 Display case of pottery
13 Head of a coyote
14 Vessel showing the perforation
   technique
15 Vessel from Tenayuca

(Objects and areas of the most
interest)

When the Teotihuacán civilization was in its final stage of decadence, new groups from the north emerged in the Central Plateau. As time passed, it was these groups that converged into what we now know as the Toltecs who developed their own culture from their capital city Tula, in the state of Hidalgo.

Existing centers, such as Xochicalco, Cholula and Cacaxtla became more important as a result, and further new centers emerged such as Teotenango and Tula, as mentioned before. These people were more inclined to militarism, a general characteristic of the early Postclassic period (850-1250 AD).

Xochicalco means the"Place of the House of Flowers"and is located in the state of Morelos, southeast of Cuernavaca. It seems that the most illustrous personage of Ancient Mexico came from this region. His name was Ce Acatl Topiltzin and is more well known as Quetzalcóatl.

The feather serpent pyramid is situated at the top of the hill. It is covered with bas-reliefs that combine many of the elements from the Central Plateau of Mexico and the Mayan

area. These contain a series of hieroglyphs whose interpretation is still controvertial but suggest calendar adjustments. There is also a ball-court with its scoring rings, similar to Tula. Among the most important finds, there are the three outstanding Xochicalco steles depicting the more important changes and events of this cultural area.

During the height of the Teotihuacán civilization, Cholula was the capital city of a parallel culture in Puebla. The Puebla and Mexico Valleys formed part of the Teotihuacán state and after the fall of Teotihuacán as a cultural center, Cholula began a new stage of a predominantly own culture.

Replica of part of the *Coatepantli wall* from Tula, Hidalgo, which shows a serpent devouring a nearly fleshless being.

TULA

There is no doubt that the Toltecs revolutionized many of the architectonic norms in vogue at the time in Mesoamerica. One of those, and perhaps one of the most important, was the "open space" concept.

One of the two largest pyramids situated at the same level as the central plaza was completely divested of its finishing layer except one simple slab at the base of the stonemasonry stairway enclosure. This indicates that it was dedicated to Venus. The other pyramid, simply named building B, or Temple of Tlahuizcalpantecutli, is rectangular and composed of five stepped sections. The upper part of these were originally covered with decorated panels of a procession of jaguars and coyotes. In the center there were eagles and vultures devouring hearts, intersected with mythical beings who emerge from the jaws of a feathered serpent.

The strong personality of the Toltecs produced magnificent monuments and sculptures of the finest quality in Tula. Fine examples, are the great serpentshaped columns, whose heads rest on the ground and their up-turned tails support the lintel beams of the entrance to the temple. Furthermore, the enormous atlantes or caryatides are outstanding both for their size of 460 m. high and for their remarkable sculpture and workmanship. They are built of four great stones assembled together with a central pin. The bas-reliefs decorating the panels of the pyramids are noted for their accomplished workmanship and likewise the famous representations of Chac-mool.

THE CULT OF QUETZALCOATL

In order to support and strengthen their mythology, men of this period claimed its creation to Quetzalcóatl. The cult to this deity was the most important in the Early Postclassic period.

They believed in and spread the legend in which Quetzalcóatl supposedly descends to the underworld with the purpose of creating mankind and to rescue the precious bones; but Mictlantecutli, the god of death, firmly opposes and assigns him various difficult missions, which seemed hard to accomplish. At last, Quetzalcóatl, with the help of his twin brother Xólotl, comes out victorious in his fight against Mictlantecutli. Quetzalcóatl does penance by bleeding his virile member over the precious bones' ashes, thus creating life in the Fifth Sun. Because of this, man is called "Macehualli", which means "Worthy by the sacrifice of the gods". Attributed to Quetzalcóatl the creation of mankind of our era, we can therefore understand the significance of this god within their religion and culture.

The religion of these militaristic societies continued to be politheistic and the deities inherited from Teotihuacán, such as Huehuetéotl were added to others like Quetzalcóatl, the Feathered Serpent whose cult extended throughout the Central Plateau and even beyond the frontiers. We see it in Xochicalco, Cholula and Tula where it reached its maximum expression during the reign of Topiltzin.

Sculpture representing *the man Quetzalcóatl*. Origin, Mexico City, Federal District.

61

THE CHANGE OF POWER

During the decline of the great theocratic Mesoamerican centers, there was already a warfaring spirit noticeable in the mural paintings of Cacaxtla, in the Xochicalco reliefs and the Tula atlantes or caryatides. Quetzalcóatl regained importance at the fall of Teotihuacán and became more associated with his military power, knowledge, forced labor and tribute than with necromancy. There were changes in the focus power of but also politically and socially. These were expressed in the form of economic and social controls, established by different ethnnic or racial groups.

There was a belief in life after death and there was a cult to the dead, as well. Related to this cult, it is common to find burials linked to temples and shrines and, based on the burial findings, there is evidence of human sacrifice, which included craneal deformation in vertical sectioning and tooth mutilation by filing.

The duality concept which was so important at that time is implicit in the morning star cult, known as Tlahuizcalpantecuhtli, "Lord of Dawn". However, being also the "Evening Star", it is called Xólotl, as well. In both cases, it is either Venus or Quetzalcóatl, the dual deity known as "Naxitl", the four-footed. Xólotl, the dog, is also called "Celestial Ray or Fire", precious twin, linked to the sacrifice of Quetzalcóatl so as to create the "Fifth Sun" and to the making of new mankind. Discoverer of maize and inventor of the calendar, Quetzalcóatl is identified at the same time as a deity of the cyclic time, of rain as well as Lord of Time.

ECONOMY

One of the richest supply sources available to the Toltecs was their subjugation of other nations through political organization. This allowed them to take advantage of the tributary work force from other regions and, moreover to complement their economy with the tributary products for their successful development. The inhabitants of the ancient city of Tula needed to intensify their cultivation of basic products such as maize and beans. This they achieved by irrigation systems. The supply of products foreign to the region such as cotton, tropical fruits, green stone, shell, feathers, etcetera was obtained through commerce with other areas of Mesoamerica. Thus, they were able to exchange this produce in the local market, held every twenty days, in other words,every month in the Mesoamerican calendar.

Plumbate vessel with a turkey shaped handle. From Acayuca, Hidalgo.

Scale model of the *main temple in Tenayuca*. The Aztecs adopted the innovation of two main temples, one for each deity.

THE CHICHIMECAS OF XOLOTL

According to the chronicles, the city of Tula was abandoned by its governors in 1165 AD until the XV th, century, when it was reinhabited by a group of Chichimecas contemporary with the Tenochtitlán Mexicas. This group gave no thought to the splendor of the buildings in the ceremonial center which they destroyed, but built their houses over the ruins. On top of Ball court II in Tula, there are remains of some of these houses, braziers, and miniature vessels of typical Mexican manufacture.

The size and orientation of the ball court situated on the west of the great plaza in Tula, is similar to those found in Chichen Itzá. Various offerings were found testifying to the period of the Mexica occupation. These include a polychromed brazier, incense burners, figurines of gods and musicians. Thanks to these, excavations and historical sources, it was proved that this center was inhabited by another group unlike the previous inhabitants.

The chief of this Chichimeca group was called Xólotl who, after guiding his followers to Tula and making them burn the buildings, led them to the eastern parts of the valley of México. He established his kingdom in Tenayuca from where they dominated the surrounding vicinity during the first half of the XIII century AD. The later predominating cultural elements of the Mexicas developed precisely from here.

Tenayuca means in náhuatl "Walled Place" and it was here that, for the first time, the base to a double temple was built to offer homage to two deities simultaneously. This idea was adopted later by the Mexicas when they built the Great Temple in Tenochtitlán.

The building was surrounded by a wall of serpents, half of which are painted in blue and the rest in black. These colors are related to the cardinal points.

Seeing the splendor emerge from the effort of his people, Quetzalcóatl, Ce Acatl Topiltzin said, "You will be the Toltecs, the builders, the designers. Our fame will extend throughout the earth and soon all Anáhuac will come to admire and learn".

Plumbate Figure of a warrior decorated with mother of pearl incrustations. From Tula Hidalgo.

65

HALL 7. THE MEXICA

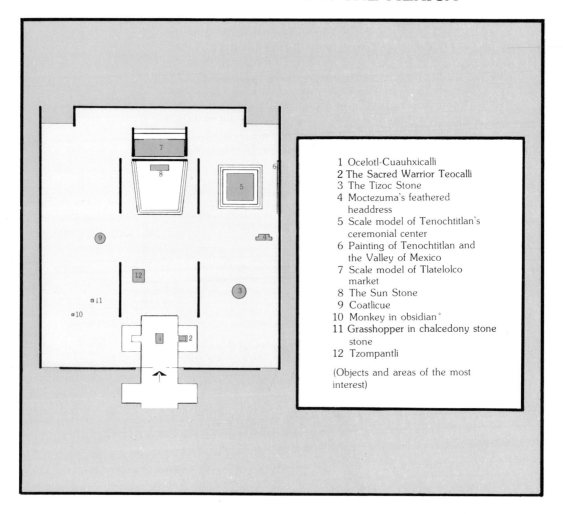

1 Ocelotl-Cuauhxicalli
2 The Sacred Warrior Teocalli
3 The Tizoc Stone
4 Moctezuma's feathered
   headdress
5 Scale model of Tenochtitlan's
   ceremonial center
6 Painting of Tenochtitlan and
   the Valley of Mexico
7 Scale model of Tlatelolco
   market
8 The Sun Stone
9 Coatlicue
10 Monkey in obsidian
11 Grasshopper in chalcedony stone
   stone
12 Tzompantli

(Objects and areas of the most
interest)

In the 13th century the Aztecs or Mexica established themselves in a beautiful region with a temperate climate and surrounded by mountains that were always covered with forests. They settled down amid the central lake zone of the Valley of Mexico, an area of 8000 square kilometers.

This group was not native to central Mexico but originally came from a region on the periphery of Mesoamerica, a site called Aztlán, "place of whiteness." According to some scholars this is located in the lake region of Yuriria-Cuitzeo in the Bajío area.

When Europeans reached the New World in the 16th century, they were surprised at the degree of economic and political power the Mexica had attained. By the time Cortés and his followers arrived, this group had used military force to subjugate other indigenous nations, exacting tribute payments from them and forming a prosperous state that the Spaniards called the "Aztec Empire."

In Mesoamerica, especially in the central region, a cultural development took place that can be appreciated through the study of its archaeology and ethnohistory. This shows us how the ancient peoples of Mexico first lived in small village communities, where they perfected their agricultural techniques. Later on they experimented with forms of government that evolved from the religious centers, and through social organization they were able to bring the communities under their control. This all brought about the emergence of states, such as the Teotihuacán state at the beginning, and finally that of the Mexica. From the time of Tula, the main activity of these states was warfare, and the process culminated with the Mexica, who inherited the entire Mesoamerican tradition, adding to it their own cultural traits. The sum total of the Mesoamerican heritage combined with their own special features formed what we call the Aztec civilization.

The most outstanding aspects of Aztec culture and society are shown in the Mexica Hall of the Museum.

Mural of the Central Mexican Plateau, by Luis Covarrubias.

67

The founding of the city of Tenochtitlán. In 1325 A.D., an indigenous group led by Tenoch found the predestined sign of an eagle on a cactus.

By the time the Aztecs arrived in the Valley of Mexico, the great prehispanic lake had divided into a series of smaller lakes and lagoons covering a wide area. Some of the most important ones were Texcoco, Chalco, Xaltocan, Xochimilco, Zumpango and San Cristobal. The largest one was Texcoco, which had a few large islands in the western part. It was on these that the Mexica founded their city of Tenochtitlan which as time went on, became a powerful metropolis dominating a vast tributary state that reached from the Gulf to the Pacific coasts and from the Bajío to Oaxaca.

The Aztecs began their pilgrimage in the year "One Flint Knife", 1116 A.D., and they temporarily settled in various places enroute. Their final settlement was in Chapultepec or Grasshopper Hill. Here they built defensive constructions and made terraces for cultivation.

Once they were established in this site they entered into conflict with people of the valley, mainly with the Tecpanecas, the Culhuas, and the Xaltomecas, who joined forces and overthrew the Mexica, whom they captured and took as prisoners-of-war to Culhuacán. There, the Mexica formed family and cultural ties with the Culhuas through marriage, and in time the newcomers began to consider themselves as descendants of the Toltecs, the alleged founders of Culhuacán. Later on they were turned out by the Culhuas and were left to roam in the marshy scrubland of the lake. There they found the omen which indicated where they should definitely settle. The sign was an eagle devouring a serpent on top of a cactus. It was in that spot that they founded their capital, Mexico-Tenochtitlán, in 1325 A.D.

In general the physical appearance of these people was similar to the other groups of the Central Plateau. They had a tawny complexion with tones varying from very light to dark, plenty of straight black hair, with almost no tendency to go bald, scant beard and moustache and no body hair, dark slanting eyes with high foreheads and wide noses. We know that the average male height was 1.60 m. and 1.48 m. for the females.

The native language was Nahuatl, which belongs to the Yuto-Aztec linguistic family.

Sculpture of a young Mexica wearing a *Maxtlatl*. From Mexico City.

Calculations of the population number have varied considerably from the 16th century to the present day. We now believe that when the Spaniards arrived, there were about 2 million inhabitants in the Valley of Mexico and 250 thousand in Tenochtitlán.

Tenochtitlán and Tlatelolco were the two island cities which together occupied some 13 square km. when the Spaniards arrived in 1519. These towns represented the labor of several generations of men who had modified and increased the original terrain, converting it into the extraor dinarily beautiful city that so astounded the Spanish conquerors.

From the beginning, the Mexica leaders devised an overall plan for their capital city, dividing the terrain in four main sections corresponding to the cardinal points. These were the four main quarters known as Atzacoalco, Cuepopan, Zoquiapan and Moyotlan.

The four original quarters accommodated the different *calpullis* that had existed since the migration, and these formed smaller districts. However, this division imposed by the ruling group caused discontent amongst one section of the population, who preferred to colonize a neighboring island and there founded Tlatelolco, which was later annexed by force to Tenochtitlán, after its conquest by Axayácatl. Thus, it became the fifth district of the Aztec capital.

The most important buildings were situated in the center of the city, the headquarters and residence of the ruling group. The ceremonial precinct was in a quadrangle measuring more than 300 meters long, and was bordered by a wall decorated with serpents —the "Coatepantli"— with three entrances where the causeways of the city originated. The enormous pyramid that served as the base for the twin temples of Tláloc and Huitzilopochtli was outstanding in size. It had a double stairway flanked on either side by low solid balustrades. There were also temples for other deities: the sun, the wind, and the gods of agriculture.

There were other structures that included the ball court and the Tzompantli. This consisted of a base that held many rows of human skulls strung on wooden bars, the macabre trophes of the sacrificial killing of prisoners-of-war.

The palaces of the noblemen and *tlatoani* (governor) were located beyond the ceremonial precinct, with the open space used for public ceremonies. During the reign of Moctezuma II the Tenochtitlán market was concentrated in Tlatelolco and the original market area in Tenochtitlán was dedicated to religious ceremonies, mainly for the festival of the "volador." The farther away from the center, the smaller and simpler was the construction of palaces and houses. The craftsmen and farmers lived on the outskirts in recovered lands called "chinampas" (artificial man-made islands), and these gave the city its peculiar characteristics.

The islands were connected with the shore by means of causeways. Tenochtitlán had three main thoroughfares: Tlacopan, which was double, with an aqueduct running through the center, carrying water from Chapultepec; Ixtapalapa, which branched out to join the villages of Ixtapalapa and Coyoacán to the city, and Tepeyac. These causeways, together with the stone and wooden wall that was on the east side, served as both dikes to regulate the volume

Fleshless Coyote. The animal was very realistically carved. From Mexico City.

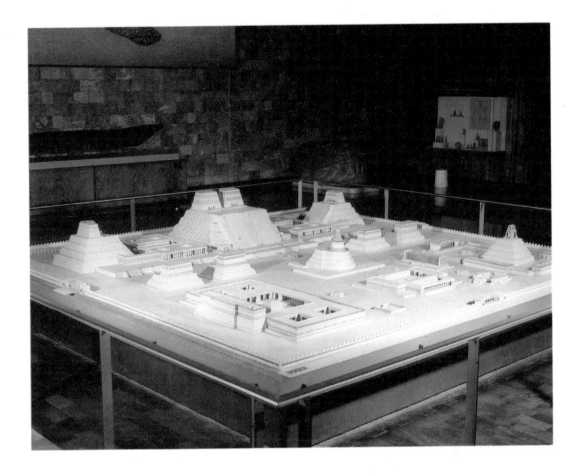

of water in the lakes, and also separated the fresh water from the brackish lakes.

Scale model of the ceremonial precinct of Mexico-Tenochtitlán. The great quadrangle area where the Mexicas erected their principal sacred buildings is well defined.

FOOD

The Mexica were a basically agricultural people and supplemented their diet by means of other activities, such as fishing, hunting and gathering. The main plants that were cultivated were the same as those in other Mesoamerican regions: maize, beans, chili peppers, squash, nopal cactus, a·kind of sage, maguey, etc. They obtained a great variety of animals from the lake which provided them with all their protein needs, such as frogs, salamanders, water skates, fish, ducks and herons. Furthermore, they also ate turkey, deer, and a certain type of dog that was especially raised for food called the *itzcuintli*.

ECONOMY

They had a flourishing economy due to various factors. One was the adequate control of the population work force;

71

another was intensive commerce combined with the collection of tribute payments which brought to the city abundant supplies of raw materials and products needed for the ruling classes. The final factor was the intensive exploitation of the environment.

The local exchange of merchandise mainly took place in the markets, *tianquiztli*, by the actual producers. Usually a bartering system was used, although there were certain objects that played a role similar to money, such as fine cloth, little copper axes, and especially cacao beans. When the Spaniards arrived, the most famous market in all Mesoamerica was the one in Tlatelolco.

SOCIAL STRUCTURE

The state established strict military ranks for the army in which the *macehual* (commoner) who was outstanding in warfare could achieve a privileged social status similar to the nobility. In this way the Aztecs induced the people to expand the national territory through conquest.

Scale model of Tlatelolco market where the activities of the market and details of every day life are vividly demonstrated.

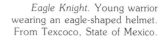

The population was organized from the very beginning into wards or *calpullis*, which were the basic cells of the Aztec state. The socio-economic organization of these units was based on family ties. They lived within an established area with communal lands cultivated by its members, and were self-sufficient. They also had their own rulers, guards, priests and teachers. Actually, the society was divided into two classes: the nobility —*pipiltin*— and the commoners —*macehualtin*—.

One of the characteristics of the Mexica civilization was its specialization in crafts which allowed certain groups of the population to dedicate themselves to the full time production of consumer articles for the ruling class and for commerce. Metalurgy developed, particularly in gold, silver and copper, using techniques such as "lost wax", casting, laminates, filigree, etc. Unfortunately, nearly all of the most valuable objects were melted down by the conquerors, however a few items were saved.

The Sun Stone. Extraordinary
monument of Mexican
archaeology.

CERAMICS

Mexica pottery shows a variety of forms and decorations, including the following types: orange with decorative motifs in black; highly polished red, and polychrome pottery that was brought from the Puebla-Tlaxcala region. Its characteristic forms are two-tiered plates, *molcajetes* (grater bowls), goblets, pitchers, *comales*, jars, etcetera.

Sculpture in stone was the artistic medium in which the Mexica excelled, producing pieces of extraordinary size and quality. Examples of this are seen in the imposing statue of Coatlicue, the Sun Stone, and the delicate carving in green stone of a squash.

RELIGION

Like all Mesoamerican peoples, the Aztecs believed that everything that existed was an integrated part of the magical-religious universe. That is to say, they thought that all aspects of life were ordained by divine will.

In the Mexica era, the religious phenomena were the result of a fusion of elements from different origins that included very ancient cults, such as the god of fire, and tribal deities were also incorporated, mainly Huitzilopochtli and Camaxtli.

Religion was also interrelated with various philosophical trends explaining the origins of the world and of life. This begins with a female-masculine duality, identified with the gods Ometecuhtli and Omecihuatl, who were the creators of all that exists. Their image of the universe was that of a space formed by the four cardinal points and its center.

Following page.
Group of ceramics, showing the variety of Aztec pottery: bowls, jars, pitchers, etc.

Nose ornament. Laminated gold in the shape of a stylized butterfly From Mexico City.

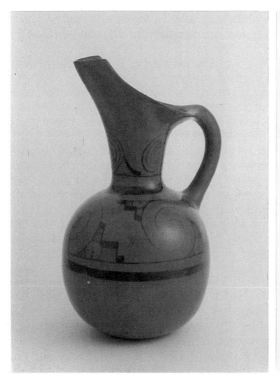

Disk. This is one of the few objects made of feathers still remaining from pre-conquest times. This represents the read of an eagle. From the State of Hidalgo.

Following page.
Coatlicue. Monumental sculpture of the earth goddess. Origin, Mexico City.

They also thought that the world and man himself had been created several times, and it was from this concept that the myth of the five cosmogonic Suns or eras developed. They believed that they were now living in the fifth Sun, Ollin-Tonatiuh, the "Sun of Movement."

The principal gods associated with the creation of life were Tezcatlipoca and Ehecatl-Quetzalcóatl, patrons of darkness and the wind, respectively. The Sun was Tonatiuh, the moon Meztli, and the earth was conceived as an old woman, Coatlicue, mother of all the gods and all mankind. The earth was also conceived as Tlaltecuhtli, a monstrous being who was always prepared to devour anything that died.

One of the characteristic features of Mexica ritual was the practice of human sacrifice. This was related to ideas about providing nourishment for the sun and for life itself, through the blood and hearts of the victims. It was also definitive proof of the power of this nation and the means by which it expanded. In sacrifice, the heart of the victim was extracted with a flint knife, but prisoners were also burned or drowned. Sometimes the flesh of the sacrificial victim was eaten in a ritual form of cannibalism, not for food but as a sort of communion between men and the god, who was personified by the victim.

Huitzilopochtli was a tribal deity related to the young god of the sun, who was triumphant in the daily battle with the

moon and the stars. To maintain him and his greatness became the pretext for military expansion.

At the head of the political organization was the *tlatoani* —"lord"— who was a type of monarch who governed for his lifetime. He was elected to this position from amongst the descendants of Acamapichtli, the first great lord. He was the head of the state, the army, and the religious hierarchy. He shared his position with the *cihuacoatl*, who was a political dignitary established during the period of Tlacaelel. Apart from him, there was a council of elders called *tlatocan*, that participated in the most important decisions. On the lower levels there was a host of public officials and employees who had particular functions, such as judges, police, guards for stores of weapons, and so forth.

As soon as the Mexicas settled in Mexico-Tenochtitlán, they elected their first *tlatoani*. The selection fell upon a prince of Culhuacán, Acamapichtli, whose enthronment marked the definite settlement of the ancient inhabitants of the Valley of Mexico.

Xochipilli. Patron god of music, song and dance.

The first three *tlatoani* were Acamapichtli, Huitzilihuitl and Chimalpopoca who governed the Mexicas whilst they were still beneath the Azcapotzalco yoke. It was during the reign of Itzcóatl that the war freeing the Mexicas from the Tecpanecas, occured. Dating from this victory, the winning allies, Tenochtitlán, Texcoco and Tlacopan, organized a political and military confederation called the Triple Alliance, which began the reconquest of the lake valley which lasted until 1434.

Izcóatl's advisor was Tlacaelal, who was the significant figure in prehispanic history. It was he who had a glimpse of Tenochtitlán glorious destiny and dictated the necessary means to consolidate her greatness. He established an official history in which this group emerged as the chosen people of the sun.

The following *tlatoanis* were, Moctezuma Ilhuicamina, Axayácatl, Tizoc and Ahuizotl. They continued the expansion of the Mexica state through military conquests.

The characteristics of the Mexica society changed with the reign of Moctezuma II, based on the efficient functioning of the tribute system. Moctezuma faced the Spanish conquerors with a fatalistic and passive attitude, not allowing his people to defend themselves against the invader.

The last Mexica rulers were Cuitláhuac and Cuauhtémoc who organized a resistance against the European attack on their city. The last *tlatoani* was captured and Tenochtitlán capitulated on August 13th, 1521.

HALL 8. OAXACA

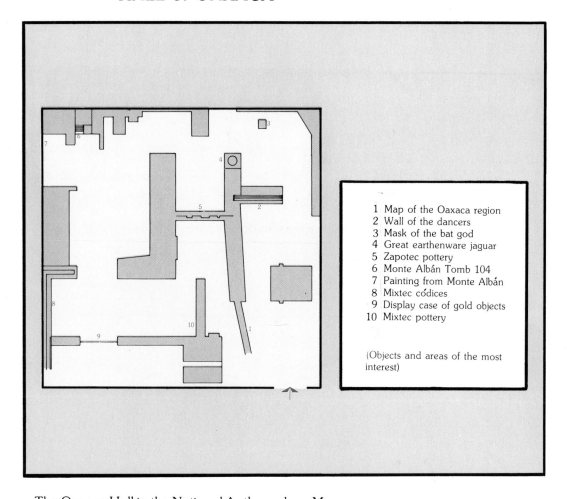

1 Map of the Oaxaca region
2 Wall of the dancers
3 Mask of the bat god
4 Great earthenware jaguar
5 Zapotec pottery
6 Monte Albán Tomb 104
7 Painting from Monte Albán
8 Mixtec códices
9 Display case of gold objects
10 Mixtec pottery

(Objects and areas of the most interest)

The Oaxaca Hall in the National Anthropology Museum, is made up of two main sections. In the first, the cultural development from the Monte Albán archaeological site is the most conspicuous. Objects on display are from various seasons of fieldwork and archaeological investigation carried out by Alfonso Caso, Ignacio Bernal and Jorge Acosta. The discovered objects have been placed in chronological order arranged within the different phases when Monte Albán was inhabited from I to V.

The following section contains a general view of the Mixteca cultural region without particular reference to archaeological sites, with the exception of the architectural example of the Yagul site. Also some aspects of the Mixteca culture have been emphasized, such as the writing in códices and the technological and craft achievements, particularly in metalurgy, stonemasonry and pottery, among others.

Remarkable *jade mask* made in several sections, representing the bat god. °

THE FIRST AGRICULTURAL COMMUNITIES

At the entrance of the Hall, there is a display-case showing the beginnings of the agricultural settlements in Oaxaca. These developed in the Etla Valley where, in about 1500 BC, in the Early Preclassic period, and were situated along the banks of the Atoyac river. The agriculture was mainly cultivating maize, beans and squash. As these communities evolved, towards 1200 BC, they showed different residential patterns that indicated a greater social stratification, for it was at this time, that buildings, specifically set aside for civic-religious activities began to be constructed. Around 900 BC these Oaxacan groups had contact with people from the Gulf Coast, as we can see by some of the magnificent objects found exchanged between both regions.

THE CLASSIC PERIOD

During the Classic period, between 200 and 800 AD, the population in the Oaxacan Valley communities increased and

Cylindrical Receptacle of earthenware, decorated with the rain god Cocijo. From Monte Albán, Oaxaca.

the building of Monte Albán continued. For its building, the Zapotecs gradually modified the topography of the hill where they placed their city. Soon they achieved a harmonic composition of volume and space by cutting away prominent rocks and hiding them beneath the constructions of platforms and buildings which formed a complex of more than 300 meters long by 200 meters wide.

CULT TO THE DEAD

The Zapotecan nobility developed an important funerary rite during the Classic period. This was the product of a cult practised by their ancestors and the religious ideas of the time. This was the reason for the construction of tombs in nearly all the buildings in which the noblemen were placed, accompanied by offerings. Tomb architecture also evolved from the oldest, more simple constructions.

Tomb 104 in Monte Albán is one of the most spectacular. The outside is made of a corniced lintel with a scapulary panel on top. In the center of this, there is a niche containing an urn representing the god Cocijo. The door is formed by a large slab covered with hieroglyphs. The chamber is rectangular with a flat roof and painted murals on the walls. Above the niche, at the back, there is a painting of the head of the god who has a large bow in his headdress. On the right side of him is a glyph 5 Turquoise and on his left, is a dignitary, possibly representing the god Xipe, carrying a bag in his hand.

Following page. Reproduction of *Tomb 104* discovered in the north of the Great Plaza in Monte Albán.

Earthenware urn representing the *god with the wide peaked helmet.* From Monte Albán, Oaxaca.

THE DECLINE OF MONTE ALBAN

The fall of the great urban Zapotec city and its gradual desertion probably began around the year 900 AD. By this time, all building construction had ceased and the greater part of the civic religious center was already in ruins, since only a few burials in the ruins have been found from this period. The disintegration of Monte Albán as the principal center of the Oaxacan Valley brought about the development of other centers in the area, such as Zaachila, Lambityeco, Cuilapan and Mitla. These were already rival cities at the founding of Monte Albán, but it was not until its decline that they grew.

Well within the Postclassic period, about 1350 BC, groups of Mixtecs arrived in the central valleys and some of them settled in the ruins of Monte Albán. The Mixtecs reused some of the Zapotec tombs to bury their chieftains. Perhaps one of the most important archaeological finds of this century, is the famous Tomb 7 of Monte Albán. It was a typical Zapotec structure with Mixtec objects found inside.

Earthenware urn representing the goddess "13 Serpent". Found in Tomb 109 in Monte Albán, Oaxaca.

MIXTEC DOMINIONS

The cultural development of the Mixtec people is displayed in the Hall and shows the advent of the Mixtec Dominions which is related in the códices. Some of the old traditions believed that the Mixtecs were guided to the mountainous area of Oaxaca by their tutelary gods through the Coixtlahuaca pass. After going through Apoala, they finally settled in Achiutla and Tilantongo where the first dynasties emerged and were registered in the Mixtec códices. The area inhabited by the Mixtecs has been divided into three subregions: the Lower Mixtec area in the west of the state, the Upper Mixtec, surrounding the first and towards the center of Oaxaca, and the Coast Mixtec, in the northeast coast of Oaxaca and part of Guerrero.

POSTCLASSIC PERIOD

The Postclassic period throughout the major part of Mesoamerica is characterized by its militarism and the Mixtec region was no exception. To the contrary, this nation was the archetype of the warfaring groups of this period. Around about the XIV century, the Mixtecs conquered the city of Zaachila causing the great Zapotec Lord to flee to the Tehuantepec region. It was from this event onwards, that the Mixtecs extended their dominions throughout the Valley of Oaxaca, mainly towards the west where they established their political capital in Cuilapan.

The Mixtecs had an ethnnic and cultural affinity but, unlike the Zapotecs, they were not organized into a great political state entity. Rather, they formed generally independant dominions which were fundamentally ruled by a military system. Professional soldiers were unknown but there were however, areas in every city which were recruiting units,

Representation of a shield or *Chimalli* in Mixtec gold with turquoise inlay. From Yanhuitlán. Oaxaca.

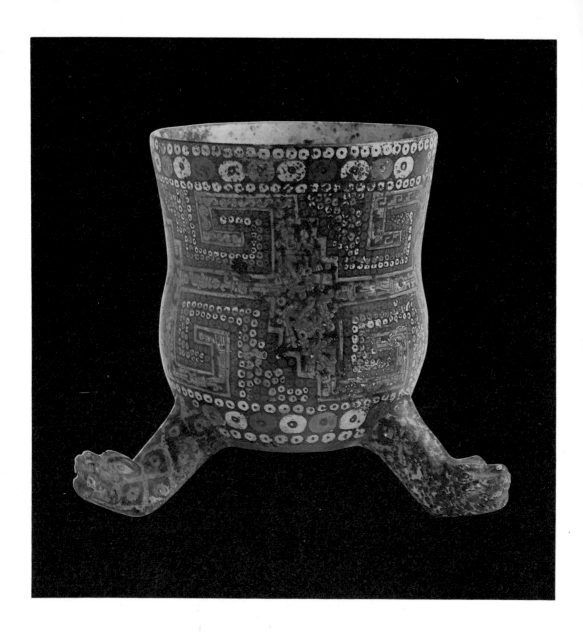

Mixtec earthenware vessel with tripod feet in the shape of a jaguar's head.

since every male member of the community was obliged to take part in combat.

METALURGY AND CERAMICS

The Mixtecs were distinguished for their craftsmanship in precious metals, mainly in gold, silver and copper. They manufactured extraordinary works of art and magnificent jewellery objects such as earplugs, noseplugs, discs, pectorals and necklaces among other things. Moreover, the Mixtec manufactured ceramics and style are famous throughout Mesoamerica and it is outstanding for its variety of shape and color. The Mixtec potters shared this tradition with those of the Cholula area and achieved magnificent examples which carried images of their gods, glyphs, geometric and fantastic motifs.

The Building of the Dancers is one of the oldest in Monte Albán since it corresponds to the first construction period. This building has a great sloping wall covered with engraved stone slabs, decorated with nude human figures in peculiar attitudes with their eyes closed, open mouthed and with glyphs.

At the entrance of the Hall there is an urn that represents the goddess "13 Serpent", since the glyph corresponding to this deity is worn on her *quechquémitl* (overblouse). This urn comes from Tomb 77 in Monte Albán. It is a large cylinder of earthenware with a modelled head of the god "Bird with Wide Beak".

Mixtec earthenware polychromed bowl with a hummingbird perched on the edge. Found in Tomb 2 in Zaachila, Oaxaca.

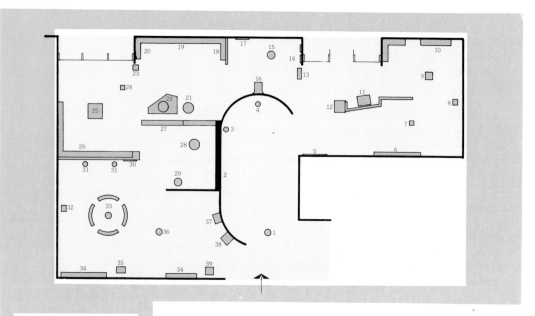

GEOGRAPHIC SITUATION

These cultures although mainly distributed along the plains of the Gulf Coast, also include some parts of the eastern Sierra Madre, in the present states of Veracruz, Tabasco, Tamaulipas part of Puebla, San Luis Potosí, Hidalgo and Querétaro.

Three cultures existed in these areas which, from south to north, included, the Olmec culture, Central Veracruz and the Huaxtec culture. The two latter cultures had developed over a long period of time for hundreds of years before Christ, to the arrival of the Spaniards in the XVIth century. However, the first culture existed for only a few centuries before Christ. The height of each culture occurred at different times, the Olmec, during the Middle Preclassic period (1200-500 BC), Central Veracruz during the Classic period (300-900 AD) and the Huaxtec in the Postclassic (900-1521 AD). This display emphasizes each one of these historical moments.

Despite the fact that these three cultures have many differences, they also have many features in common, so they have been considered within one framework. The first similarity, is that they developed in a similar geographical climate and the second, is the way in which the human groups adapted to their environment.

There is a long plain stretching from the south of Tamaulipas approximately to Campeche, which is at least 800 meters above sea level. This forms the dividing line between the temperate and hot lands. These plains have been considered an ecological unity since prehispanic times since a series of natural characteristics coincide in this area, such as the natural tropical forest vegetation which permits two harvests a year, depending on the rainfall and with the exception of the semi-arid zone of Central Veracruz. Rainfall usually exceeds 1,000 mm a year and creates enormous quantities of water that flow into a wide-bedded river system with extensive fluvial planes such as the Pánuco-Tamesí, the Papaloapan, the Coatzacoalcos and the Grijalva-Usumacinta rivers. Apart from creating lagoons and estuaries, this fluvial system also provides a means of transportation as well as food resources.

A large area of the lower terrain in these plains are great flooded flat-lands, marshes and lagoons. However, the stretch between the Pánuco river and the Papaloapan is an area of rolling, topographically well-drained hills.

Despite the fact that in past times a large part of agricultural land could not be used because it was permanently flooded, there were other very fertile areas. The alluvial plains among these were well drained like the hilly terrain.

This environment caused the population to be scattered in small groups, either hamlets, small settlements and vil-

Map of the Olmec region showing the rivers and streams irrigating the central mountainous area of the Tuxtlas.

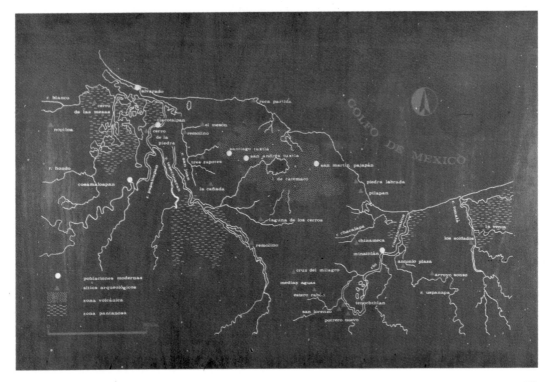

lages. There were ceremonial centers in only a few places where there was a larger nuclei of people. Although there were many centers, they never had large populations and never obtained the size and extent of those in the Central Plateau. From the Classic period on, these groups seem to have organized themselves into independant dominions which never unified into one state, unlike other cultures of ancient Mexico.

Maybe this difference lay in the fact that the agricultural system did not require a large collective system as in the Central Plateau. More over, there was no necessity for a state or a dominant class in a group whose principal activity was to increase their agricultural potencial.

THE OLMECS

The word "Olmec" means "inhabitant of the rubber region". These people lived on the Gulf Coast, south of Veracruz and part of Tabasco, during the Upper and Middle Preclassic period (1300-100 AD)

A large area of their terrain was permanently underwater or muddy. The dense and thick vegetation forced the Olmecs to find better ways of communication along the rivers and lakes.

SCULPTURE

The larger part of this area is lowland, interrupted only by the Tuxtla mountains, at an altitude of 500 meters, and from which they extracted the stone used in their sculptures. These sculptures were most frequently human figures, either in relief, or in the round, colossal heads, altars or stellae. The collosal heads and altars are unique in Mesoamerica and little is known of their exact symbolism. However, some researchers think that they may be representations of chieftains or decapitated players in the ball game. Ideas concerning the origin of the Olmec ancestors were represented in their altars.

Apart from the monumental sculpture, the Olmecs also produced a vast quantity of small sculptures in green stone such as "jade" and jadete which were used as ornaments or ceremonial objects.

The Olmecs were the people who began to assign the great importance of "jade". This green stone came to represent in Mesoamerica, the "most valuable", and was always related to the fertility concept.

TECHNOLOGY AND CERAMICS

One of the greatest technological achievements of these people was the construction of the first known water system control in prehispanic Mexico. They built a grid of drainage canals in San Lorenzo, Veracruz, whose main canal measures 1,674 meters long, whilst the secondary canals measure 294 meters. All these canals were built with perfectly cut and fitted stone slabs. This was, without doubt, the work of specialists.

Olmec pottery is fairly simple and made of the typical creamy clay of the Gulf Coast. There is generally little decoration with motifs mainly associated with the jaguar.

Stone sculpture of a *male figure* wearing a loin-cloth, belt and pectoral. Olmec culture of the Middle Preclassic period from San Lorenzo, Veracruz.

Colossal head in stone representing chieftains or ball game players. Olmec culture from San Lorenzo, Veracruz.

ARCHITECTURE

When the Olmec ceremonial sites were converted into the capital centers of various villages or neighboring hamlets, a new form of political organization emerged which tended to concentrate all the power and knowledge into one single group.

The most important human settlements of the Olmec culture were found in La Venta, Tabasco, Tres Zapotes and San Lorenzo-Tenochtitlán in Veracruz. These were ceremonial centers whose building reveal a precise concept of orientation. The pyramidal bases were of different shapes, either rectangular or round and were built round a central space that served as a ceremonial plaza. Since the materials used were only earth or mud, their buildings never achieved a monumental scale.

RELIGION

The Olmec religion revolved around the fertility cult with the jaguar as the principal god. Religion was interlaced with the political and social organization, as in all the other Mesoamerican cultures.

SOCIAL ORGANIZATION AND KNOWLEDGE

The Olmec population was divided into social classes with their hierarchies. Some of these had access to the privileges of knowledge and dominated leading positions of priests, artists and merchants.

This was the first culture to depict a calendar system in stone, as can be seen in Stele C from Tres Zapotes, Veracruz. This stele has the oldest engraved date so far known in Mesoamerica, 31 years before Christ.

During the Preclassic period, the Olmecs presented a series of features that would form bases for the development of the great Classic period of the Mesoamerican cultures.

Earthenware vessel with representation of a jaguar face. Middle Preclassic period of the Olmec culture from the Valley of Mexico.

Offering from La Venta, Tabasco, composed of 16 figures and 6 axes in green stone. Middle Preclassic period of the Olmec culture.

CULTURE OF CENTRAL VERACRUZ

In the central area of Veracruz, different cultures were developed from the ones we find in the southern part of this area (the Olmec) or in the northern part (the Huaxtec). At the moment, we have no better name for them than that of "Cultures of Mid Veracruz", known also as "Central Veracruz" or "Tajín Style". Nevertheless, there was such a marked regional diversity which in turn produced a number of local varieties.

It could be said that this culture is bordered by the Cazones River in the north and the Papaloapan in the south; the Eastern Sierra Madre in the west and small extensions of the present States of Puebla and Oaxaca.

ARCHITECTURE

Ceremonial architecture in the center of Veracruz began at the end of the Preclassic period (800-100 BC) when a formalized religious cult already existed with an organized class of priests. The first constructions were built with burnt clay or mud and in some places covered with stone. A characteristic feature of this region was the use of oyster shells to fill in the artificial platforms and also the use of lime to cover the buildings.

Tajin with its peculiar architectonic style was built in an area of small hills with numerous buildings, sculptures and bas-reliefs. It was inhabited for many long years from the beginning of the Classic period to the beginning of the Post-classic period (100-1100 AD).

Its buildings decorated with niches, frets and overhanging cornices gave it its particular style of lightness.

SCULPTURE

The Central Veracruz sculpture, both in earthenware and stone, demonstrate some of the most highly developed artis-

Left. Painted clay *smiling figurine* depicting a dancer. The body is adorned with paint, a necklace with a bell and circular ear plugs.

Right. *Stone stele* from Tepatlaxco, Veracruz. Finely carved low relief of a ball game player dressing for the great ceremonial ball game. Classic period.

97

Left. *Stone stele* from Aparicio, Veracruz, depicting a decapitated ball game player with the blood spurting from his neck in the form of seven serpents. Classic period of the Central Veracruz culture.

Right. *Ceremonial* made in stone. These, the yokes and the axes are associated with the ball game. This representation of the arm and hand is unique in this Late Classic period of the Central Veracruz culture.

tic tendancies in ancient Mexico. In the Classic period, the smiling figurines are an exceptional example. Can we discover something of the origins of the Olmecs in the concept of the smile? Does it originate in the cult to fertility which was expressed by the lively enjoyment of dancers and musicians?

At the end of the Classic period, earthenware products achieved surprising progressive levels, such as those manifested in the life-size human figures found in the Zapotal and Cocuite sites and the representation of the Old God of Fire from Las Mesas in Veracruz.

Among the quantities of minor stone sculptures from the Classical period, the most peculiar is the "yoke-axe-palm" complex, which was closely related to the ball-game and the cult to the dead.

The ball game was a feature associated with the religion of Mesoamerica and also served as a place where a series of stonemasonry elements were developed, many of which can be appreciated in the various Tajín courts. The same can be said of the bas-reliefs in Tajín and the Aparicio stele showing a decapitated man.

The principal example of Postclassic (850-1521 AD) architecture is found in the capital of the Totonac dominions, Cempoala. This is a city which reflects a certain amount of influence from the Central Plateau.

When the Spaniards arrived in Mesoamerica in 1519 AD, Cempoala was the first great indigenous city that they encountered. Both, Hernán Cortés and his soldiers were astounded by the beauty of its arts and architecture.

HUAXTEC CULTURE

The original area occupied by the Huaxtecs was the north Gulf Coast, which included the present states of Veracruz, San Luis Potosí, Hidalgo and Tamaulipas with a small part of Puebla and Querétaro. In the present day, the Huaxtecs still exist but they inhabit a very much reduced area in a small part of Veracruz and San Luis Potosí. Their original location extended through a variety of climates and natural scenery, from the hot unhealthy climate of the coast and coastal plains, to the heights of the Eastern Sierra Madre, the Potosin Central Plateau and the rugged mountainous region of Tamaulipas.

The Huaxtec language belongs to the Mayan family although separated from them some 3,500 years ago under the pressure of other people speaking different languages among them. Some 40,000 indigenous people of Veracruz, San Luis Potosí and Hidalgo still speak this language to the present day.

CERAMICS

During the Classic period, the Huaxtec pottery acquired its own particular and definite characteristics. The creamy colored fine paste clay began to be used and anthropomorphic shapes began to emerge. In the later Postclassic period these handicrafts showed greater affinity with the rest of Mesoamerica without losing its own identity of wine or black colored decoration.

Earthenware vessel in the shape of a woman with red and black paint. Late Classic period of Huaxtec culture.

MINOR ARTS

One of the materials that the Huaxtecs became masters in was shell craft. There are innumerable examples of cut sea snail shells used as pectorals. Many of them are beautifully engraved with religious and mythical motifs that rival those found in the códices of other Mesoamerican groups. This artistic handcraft achieved its height during the Classic period and is particularly noteworthy when one considers the tools used.

SCULPTURE

As all the prehispanic peoples on the Gulf Coast, the Huaxtecs were particularly good stone sculptors. Their first works belonging to the Classic period, was at a time when they were still relatively isolated from the rest of Mesoamerica. Yet, they are pecularly similar to other marginal cultures, such as those in the West of Mexico. The religious beliefs surrounding the origin of life through the concept of fertility, are depicted in stone. These show female representations with their hands placed over the womb, adolescent males symbolizing maize together with male figures clearly indicating their sex. The greatest works of art were produced during the Postclassic period of which there are several fine examples including the Tamuín Adolescent from San Lusi Potosí, the Priest from El Naranjo, Veracruz and the Jalpan Adolescent from Querétaro.

The Huilocintla stone from Veracruz, exemplifies the hybrid style which emerged in Central Veracruz. This sculpted figure includes Huaxtec elements and shows how the Huaxtec culture infiltrated into the great Mesoamerican myths.

RELIGION AND GODS

The Huaxtec religion was impregnated with the simplicity of its origins when the cult to the dead and fertility were the

The Huilocintla Stone, Veracruz, depicting one of the god Quetzalcóatl-Ehécatl's High priests. Postclassic period of the Huaxtec culture.

Right. Front view of a stone sculpture known as the Youth. Early Postclassic period of the Huaxtec culture.

main ideas. It became more complex later with the Mesoamerican influence. Generally speaking, the Huaxtec gods are associated with the concept of fertility and a cult to the moon. The god Quetzalcóatl-Ehécatl is Huaxtec in origin and as his particular symbol, wears a cut sea-snail shell dedicated to the god of wind.

During the late Postclassic period in the Central Plateau, the Mexica culture adopted some of the Huaxtec gods, such as Quetzalcóatl-Ehécatl and Tlazolteotl.

A large part of the Huaxtec territory became subjected for a short period to the Tenochtitlán empire, during the reign of the Mexica lord Ahuizotl. However, by the time the Spaniards arrived in 1519, the Huaxtecs were relatively independent. They still retained important geographical sites within territories, such as Castillo de Teayo, Veracruz. Huaxtec sculptures clearly showing Mexica elements came from this site.

HALL 10. THE MAYAS

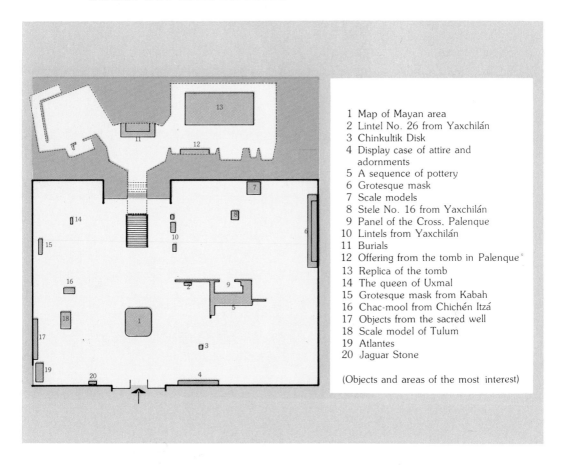

1 Map of Mayan area
2 Lintel No. 26 from Yaxchilán
3 Chinkultik Disk
4 Display case of attire and
  adornments
5 A sequence of pottery
6 Grotesque mask
7 Scale models
8 Stele No. 16 from Yaxchilán
9 Panel of the Cross, Palenque
10 Lintels from Yaxchilán
11 Burials
12 Offering from the tomb in Palenque°
13 Replica of the tomb
14 The queen of Uxmal
15 Grotesque mask from Kabah
16 Chac-mool from Chichén Itzá
17 Objects from the sacred well
18 Scale model of Tulum
19 Atlantes
20 Jaguar Stone

(Objects and areas of the most interest)

The Mayan culture flourished within a vast geographical area which stretched from the Tupilco Lagoon in Tabasco, to the Ulúa Valley in Honduras and the Lempa river in El Salvador. It covered approximately 400,000 square kilometers including a large area of southeast Mexico. It incorporates the greater part of Tabasco and Chiapas, the entire states of Yucatán, Campeche and Quintana Roo, Belize, Guatemala and the western fringes of Honduras and El Salvador, Central America.

The cultural development of the Mayas began some 1,500 years before Christ and this extensive area is still inhabited today by their descendants. We can name some of the present day Maya peoples like the Choles, the Lacandones, the Yucatecans, the Chorties, the Tzeltales and the Tzolziles, among others.

The Mayas forged one of the most brilliant Mesoamerican cultures, outstanding architecture is characterized by the use

Lintel 26 from Yaxchilán, Chiapas.

of a special type of roof, the so called "false arch" or mayan vault formed by layers of stones - each layer slightly projecting inwards; the elaborated façades of the buildings; the construction of large ceremonial centers with pyramids and temples distributed around large courtyards; the custom of erecting stelae and altars commemorating different important events; their own hieroglyphic writing and a twenty based positional numerical system which implied the previous invention and use of the "zero", a prodigious development of abstract thought which the Mayans achieved centuries before it arrived in Europe from the Arabs and consequently, before the positional mathematical system was in common use in the old world.

Their knowledge in the mathematical and astronomical fields was of particular importance. They developed a ritual, or sacred calendar of 260 days and a civil calendar of 365 days. They combined both Calendars to form the Calendar Wheel or 52 year cycle which is the basis of Mayan Chronology. They calculated the lunar and Venus cycles, and were capable of predicting eclipses and making corrections in their civil calendar to adjust it to the real solar year. Some of their calculations proved to be more exact by a tenth thousand part of a day, than the present calculations using our Gregorian calendar system.

A tour through the hall shows some of the more important aspects of the Mayan culture.

ENVIRONMENT

The first part of the hall is dedicated to show the type of environment, with the help of a relief map, photographs and a painting by Luis Covarrubias showing an ideal geographical cross section of the Mayan area. The latter clearly illustrates, not only the geographical extent of the area, but also the environmental differences, climatic changes, the relief and vegetation from the mountainous high regions of the south to the calcaric lowlands that gradually lower to the sea level in the north, passing through perennial tropical forests and the alluvial planes of the central zone. We can also appreciate graphically, how the "cenotes" were formed in the semi-arid planes of Yucatán since the whole area lacks rivers, lakes and lagoons and the "cenotes" were the only natural source of water supply.

Clay female figurines from Jaina.
Campeche. Classic period
300-900 AD.

Clay figurine depicting an *important personage* from Jaina, Campeche. Classic period 300-900 AD.

PHYSICAL FEATURES OF THE MAYAS

There are innumerable representations of the ancient Maya, in stone, stucco, mural paintings and ceramics, which show us their physical features it is remarkable to watch how those features have persisted through the centuries in their present-day descendants. The Mayas are short, with wide heads, sparse and straight hair. Their faces are wide with prominent cheek bones, well defined lips, wide straight noses, almond shaped, or slightly slanted eyes due to the heavy eyelids.

Excellent examples of the Maya physical features can be seen in the anthropomorphic decorations on Lintel 26 of Yaxchilán and the extraordinary stucco mask found in Palenque, Chiapas.

These human representations of the Mayas also show a series of artificial deformations that were practiced in ancient times to distinguish them from other groups, or indicate social rank or position, or to achieve an ideal of physical beauty. The most important deformation practiced which should be pointed out was that of the head. According to historical sources, a few days after the birth of a child, two planks were placed in the front and back of the head and securely tied, deforming the skull to produce the classical profile which we observe in the human representations.

They also practiced teeth deformation by the re-shaping or the filing of the teeth to apply incrustations of other material such as jade or pirite.

Judging by the frequent scarring and thick healed wounds found on human representations, scarification was another popular type of deformation. Again, according to historical sources, this was achieved by lightly cutting the skin forming a previously chosen design and the wound purposely infected to produce thick scar tissue leaving a permanent decoration. Although the records mention that scarification was performed on various parts of the body, almost all the existing examples are on the face, with an enormous variety of designs.

GARMENTS AND ADORNMENTS

The stone and stucco sculptures and the clay figures show the different physical types and artificial deformations practiced by the Mayas. They are also excellent documents showing the dress and adornments differenciating the social classes or the activities and professions of the ancient Maya society. Furthermore, they illustrate a series of handcrafts which, as they were made of perishable materials such as leather, feathers, textiles, basket weaving, have not withstood the test of time and therefore provide us with invaluable information.

We can also see that they used cotton materials for their garments, animal skins, enormous and feathered headdresses, necklaces, earplugs, noseplugs, rings, bracelets, etc. of very different materials such as jade, shell, bone, obsidian, copper, gold, etcetera.

Painting showing the social pyramid.

SOCIAL ORGANIZATION

Judging by the variety of attire and from the historical sources, we can deduce that the ancient Mayan society was divided into social classes. We can distinguish four different groups divided into two general categories.

The ruling class was formed by the high priests and noblemen. The main civil chieftain, the "Halach Uinic", the great high priest, "Ahaucán", the supreme military chief or "Nacón" and the other noblemen, civil functionaries, the militia and minor priests belonged to this class.

The dominated class was composed of plebeians and slaves. The majority of the population included farmers, craftsmen, warriors, merchants, etc. The slaves were the lowest rank of the social scale and were used as beasts of burden, which made them come to be an important commercial commodity.

Left. Vessel decorated with symbolic motifs.

Right. *Female figurine* of clay depicting a high society lady, from Jaina, Campeche. Classic period 300-900 AD.

From the material or economic point of view, the dominating priest class was a non productive, parasitic class but at the same time, it was the medium through which the people could communicate with the gods. They acquired remarkable scientific knowledge which provided the priesthood with great power and wisdom. The bulk of the population provided the economic stability of the community, they built the temples and pyramids, as well as manufacturing all sorts of utility items and ornamental objects.

RELIGION AND COSMOVISION

Religion and religious ceremonies to the gods played an extremely important part in the life of the Mayas. As we continue our tour through the hall we will come accross a variety of objects. One of the display-cases contains musical instruments such as, whistles, ocarinas, flutes, rattles in the shape of clay figurines together with bone rasps. These musical instruments remind us that not only music, but also dance played an important part in their ceremonies. Another display-case shows us various representations of some of the gods, high priests or noblemen before altars or thrones, together with some of the ritual objects.

To the Mayas, man was created from maize. The principal creator was Hunab Kú, but there is not one representation found of him. Although they seemed to have had a great number of gods, some were, for obvious reasons, more important than others, since they were associated with natural elements, such as the sun, fertility and water. The most important god in the Maya pantheon is a celestial god Itzam Ná "sky dew". He personifies the creator principle. Then there is Chaac the god of rain, Kinich Ahau the sun god, Yxchel the moon goddess. Yum Kax, the young god of maize, Ah Puch, the god of death and many others similar to the gods in the rest of Mesoamerica, but with different names.

The ritual to the gods included other features besides the music and dance that we have mentioned. It included fast-

Stele No. 18 from Yaxchilán, Chiapas.

Turquoise and shell mosaic Disk° found in the substructure of the Castle in Chichén Itzá. Postclassic period 900-1521 AD.

ing, abstinence and sacrifices. The latter went from simple offerings of food and objects, to self sacrifices which included the bleeding of certain parts of the body to offer to the gods, and the ultimate sacrifice of humans.

CERAMICS

On the left towards the front, a long display-case shows us the development of pottery. Here we can see how the different shapes, techniques and decorative motifs evolved. We see the older more simple vessels with one or two colors, from the first periods (Preclassic 1500 BC - 150 AD and Proto-classic 150 -300 AD) up to the most complicated,elegant, and beautifully polychromed, with symbolic, zoomorphic and anthropomorphic motifs from the period of the highest cultural development (Classic 300-900 AD).

THE CLASSIC ART

There are a great number of objects throughout the Hall either in display-cases or on isolated pedestals, that demonstrate the magnificence of the classic art in its varied expressions, either in sculpture, stonecutting, ceramics, jade, bone and shell work etc. Each item is a work of art of its kind, for the delicacy of its shape, the appropriate technique and its fine finish.

Particularly noteworthy are the lintels and the stelae of Yaxchilán, Chiapas and the Tablet of the Cross from Palenque. They not only demonstrate a beauty and remarkable skill in decorative reliefs, but are also impressive historic

Following page. Male head made in stucco and found as an offering in the Palenque tomb.

110

because of the historic importance of the events registered (or recorded) on them, which are part of maya history in general and of the sites already mentioned —Palenque and Yaxchilán—. Their symbolic representations and hieroglyphic inscriptions have been studied extensively and they have contributed considerable progress in the deciphering of the Maya hieroglyphic writing.

ARCHITECTURE

There are various models and mounted photos of some of the Mayan sites and temples showing us some of the characteristic architectural features of this culture. The environmental differences within the Mayan area was a determining factor in the formation of regional styles. However, there are certain features common to all the sites. For example, the use of the "Mayan vault" or false arch, the "acrópolis", quadrangles, the extremely tall pyramidal bases crowned with temples with "roof combs" and the "palaces"

In this section there is also the restored enormous central grotesque mask, of Kinich Ahau. This sun god has other sculptoric elements either side which include two representations of ancient gods related to fire. They are part of an artificial platform that supported some structure but we do not know its place of origin. It is one of the latest important adquisitions in the Maya Hall. It was recuperated in thousands of pieces which had unfortunately been sadly damaged by the criminal looters of the nation's cultural heritage. It is also an example of the use the Mayas gave to the grotesque mask as an architectural element. Furthermore, it is a fine example of the excellent work executed by our restorers.

FUNERARY CUSTOMS

There is a staircase leading down into the section demonstrating the funerary customs practiced by the Mayas ending with the most sumptuous of them all. This is the Royal Tomb or funerary chamber found inside the pyramid of the Temple of Inscriptions in Palenque, Chiapas. The reproduction is life-size and demonstrates that, at least in this case, some of the Mesoamerican pyramids were also used as tombs for some important personage. The opulence of the offerings mainly in jade, rival the beauty and symbolism of the stone and stucco reliefs that decorate the walls of the crypt and the tombstone covering the sarcophagus.

Leaving the tomb, there is a large door leading to the garden where there are some reproduction stelae from Calkmul, Piedras Negras, Quiriguá and Copán. There is also a life-size reproduction of a temple from Hochob, demonstrating the architectonic style called "Chenes" from the northern region.

This is characterized by the entire facade of the temple being a huge grotesque mask of the god of rain Chaac or Itzam Ná, god of the sky. The other life-size temple reproduction, contains the most important mural paintings so far found within the Mayan zone and these came from Bonampak.

Sculpture of the type known as *Chac-mool* found in Chichén Itza. Postclassic period 900-1521 AD.

THE NORTHERN REGION AND THE POSTCLASSIC PERIOD

Returning to the Hall, the visitor will find models and various objects coming from the northern Mayan region. Here, certain regional stylistic variants were developed and are noticeable in both architecture and other aspects.

There was a profuse use of fine stone mosaic work to decorate the façades of the temples. We can also observe that objects were imported from other regions of Mexico and Central America, showing the wide extent and increase in commerce from the Classic period to the arrival of the

Spaniards (Postclassic period 900-1521 AD). Most of the objects on display, correspond to this last period.

With the invading groups that arrived from the Central Plateau, the Mayan culture suffered severe foreign influences. The Toltecs, Putunes and Itzáes, led by Quetzalcóatl-Kukulkán, break into Maya history, imposing their culture in the Yucatán peninsula. Among the most remarkable and well known pieces found in the last part of this Hall, we find a Chac-mool type sculpture and the "Atlantes" from Chichén Itzá which are significant proofs of this development within the Mayan culture. There are other examples of stone sculpture, metal objects found in the Sacred "Cenote" (kind of well) in Chichén Itzá and beautifully worked disks in turquoise, coral, shell and pearl mosaics.

The invasion also marked the beginning of decadence. Internal conflicts, rebellions and enemities divided and weakened the Mayan territorial unity. Militarism was imposed and at the same time it seems that artistic and ceremonial activities ceased. The local pottery faded and more imported pottery was used. The architecture and sculpture were of poor quality and in general, it was a propitious moment for the imminent arrival of the Spaniards and the ensueing conquest.

Sculpture known as the *Atlante* type, from Chichén Itzá. Postclassic period 900-1521 AD.

HALL 11. CULTURES OF NORTH MEXICO

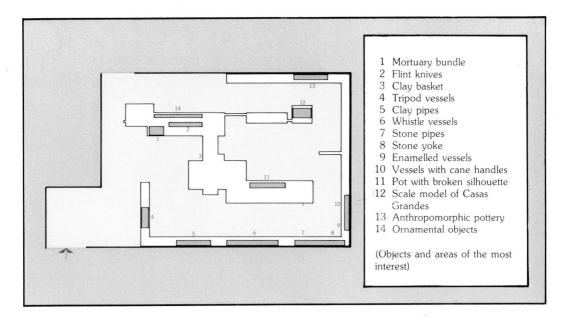

1 Mortuary bundle
2 Flint knives
3 Clay basket
4 Tripod vessels
5 Clay pipes
6 Whistle vessels
7 Stone pipes
8 Stone yoke
9 Enamelled vessels
10 Vessels with cane handles
11 Pot with broken silhouette
12 Scale model of Casas Grandes
13 Anthropomorphic pottery
14 Ornamental objects

(Objects and areas of the most interest)

The Hall containing Cultures in the North of Mexico offers a general panorama of the most representative communities found in this region. These were the results of several thousand years of cultural development in inhospitable territories that determined the expansion, or otherwise, of its inhabitants.

At the entrance of the Hall there is a presentation showing the evolution of the different cultural traditions within their geographic areas from 10,000 BC to the middle of the XIX century.

THE DESERT CULTURE

Further on, some of the Desert Culture aspects are shown. This was an ancient tradition that emerged in the west of North America when the climate changed at the end of the Pleistocene era when the ice cap of the last glaciation retreated. This obliged man to look for new economic means and caused him to exploit the resources of an arid environment. We have found caves and open-air camps on the Plateau in the North of Mexico. These remains, always near a water source, indicate settlements of hunting-gathering groups who had been pushed to the desert regions.

In certain areas, these groups managed to domesticate wild plants, among which was maize. After thousands of

Beautiful *ceramic piece* from
Casas Grandes, Chihuahua.

years of experimenting, these became the basis of their agriculture.

MESOAMERICA FRINGES

The following section, indicates the different agricultural cultures found in the northern frontiers of Mesoamerica. Here we find traces of Mesoamerican features mixed with regional elements characterized by the particular local groups.

The Mesoamerican expansion towards the north began in the Upper Preclassic period (800-100 BC) but reached its furthest extension about 1000 AD and included the areas round the mouth of the Pánuco river the Tamaulipas Sierra, the Potosino Plateau, part of Zacatecas and Durango, to the Mayo river in Sinaloa. After this time, due to various factors, either climatic, social, political or economic, the northern frontier retreated and the farming communities abandoned these regions which were once again inhabited by hunting and gathering groups called by the Mesoamericans, Chichimecas.

OASIS AMERICA

The region occupied by the present day Arizona, Nuevo Mexico, Colorado and Utah was once inhabited by groups who developed an agricultural culture in small settlements known as the Southwest or Oasis America culture. These maintained certain contact with the northwest Mesoamerica and came to establish trading routes at different times.

From as early as 3000 BC an incipient agriculture was practiced but it was not until 300 AD that the first permanent settlements appeared. Three great cultural sub-regions were identified in the Southwest: Anazazi, Hohokam and Mogollón. These appear in this Hall as a definite example of a defined culture.

CASAS GRANDES

At the end of the Hall some aspects of the Casas Grandes culture are on display. This culture developed in the northwest of the present state of Chihuahua and after 100 AD received considerable Mesoamerican influences which eventually transformed the economic, social and religious life of Casas Grandes. Paquimé, the capital of this archaeological province, controlled a commercial complex of raw materials and manufactured goods that circulated both to the north and the south. In a few years, Paquimé was converted into a great center which served as a link between Mesoamerica and the Southwest of North America.

BASKET WEAVING

Basket weaving was one of the techniques developed by the nomadic groups of the desertic region. Due to the fact that baskets were light, easily transported and replaceable, this handcraft developed innumerable shapes according to their necessities and became very successful. Various remains

Ceramic with geometric motifs from Casas Grandes.

Sometimes *zoomorphic and anthropomorphic* features were added to the geometric designs.

of basket-work have been found in the caves that were used as seasonal camps.

WEAPONS

Hunting weapons played an important part in the economy of the nomadic groups of the desertic region. Among these, was the *átlatl* or blow-gun. This permitted much easier and more efficient hunting, since they could project the dart with greater force and a further distance. The bow and arrow was introduced later but the *átlatl* was used right up to later periods.

CULT TO THE DEAD

Among some of the Desert Culture groups, it was common practice to deposit their dead in caves. Archaeologists have studied the reamins found in these caves and have been able to glean some information about the religious ideas of this culture and some of their ideas explaining "after life". The bodies were shrouded and placed in a crouching position accompanied by offerings consisting of personal objects, according to the age and sex of each individual.

POTTERY

In some of the sites that emerged in the early period on the northern boundaries of Mesoamerica such as Los Morales,

118

Guanajuato, we can observe two pottery traditions, one coming from the Valley of Mexico and another from Chupícuaro. The latter was a focal cultural point situated to the south of Guanajuato, which had considerable influence on both the cultures of the West and North Mexico. This shows that human settlements in the frontier regions maintained contact with peoples in distant regions during the Upper Classic period.

GODS

There are few representations of gods found among the north frontier people. During the Classic period (100 BC-800 AD) clay braziers were produced in the Guanajuato region and we now believe that they represent some local gods, since it seems they have a certain relationship to some of the Mesoamerican gods.

The pipe was a northern element introduced into Mesoamerica through the northeast frontier during the Classic period. Innumerable stone pipes were discovered in Cueva Vetada, San Luis Potosí, similar to those found in the southeast of the United States. Offerings were deposited in the spring head forming the Half-Moon Lagoon situated in Río Verde, San Luis Potosí. This leads us to believe, that the place was considered a sanctuary. A number of schematic anthropomorphic figurines were among the salvaged offerings. These wore headdresses and some of them have a mouth mask in the shape of a beak. Judging by their attiere, they have been associated with the ball game, since a number of structures dedicated to this activity, have also been found in the area.

The oldest *pottery* displayed only one color. Later combinations of black, white and red were used.

119

The inhabitants of Casas Grandes were excellent stonemasons. They made *mortars, axes and ornaments* of striped green stone.

MINING

The cultures developed in both the Zacatecas, Durango, the Sierra Gorda and Querétaro regions, based their economy on the exploitation of mineral sources. The Chalchihuite culture in Zacatecas, mined deposits of green stone, known as "chalchihuites", from which they produced items related to fertility, water and rain. The characteristic pottery from the first evolutionary periods is called black, scratched Michilía.

HOHOKAM CULTURE

The Hohokam people settled in the desertic zone of south Arizona along the banks of the river Ĝila and its tributaries. Thanks to explorations undertaken in the Snaketown site, we have been able to identify elements relating this culture to Mesoamerica. The same applied to the pottery in which there are similar ornamental motifs, figurines, coloring, etc. in both cultures.

POTTERY

Pottery developed late among the Anazazi groups (400-700 AD). However, as time passed, they developed their own style which can be particularly identified in the different shaped vessels and the two colored (black on white) geometric designs. Later the neighboring Mogollón region adopted the same style and in the Mimbres area it was developed into one of the most beautiful pottery of the Southwest.

ARCHITECTURE

During the Middle Period (1060 - 1340 AD), Casas Grandes developed into a city which followed the construction patterns used in the Southwest where the living quarters were built of several storeys, housing a large number of people. The building materials were adobe (mud bricks) for the walls, packed earth floors and wooden roofs that also served as the floor for the upper level.

CASAS GRANDES

Casas Grandes was an important center where raw materials were concentrated from far away places. Goods were manufactured for local consumption and to use for trade within a wide commercial field, such as in the case of shells brought from the Californian coast and turquoise from the Arizona mines.

View of the *typical architecture* used in Casas Grandes, where the walls were built of adobe brick and the floors were of packed earth.

HALL 12. WEST MEXICO

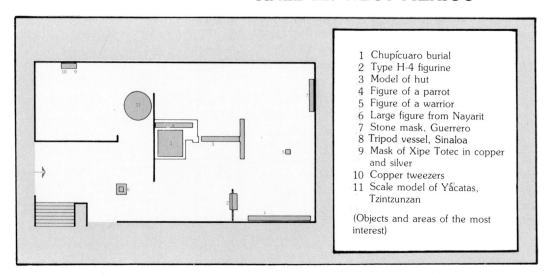

1 Chupícuaro burial
2 Type H-4 figurine
3 Model of hut
4 Figure of a parrot
5 Figure of a warrior
6 Large figure from Nayarit
7 Stone mask, Guerrero
8 Tripod vessel, Sinaloa
9 Mask of Xipe Totec in copper and silver
10 Copper tweezers
11 Scale model of Yácatas, Tzintzunzan

(Objects and areas of the most interest)

The ancient inhabitants of West Mexico occupied a large area on the Pacific Coast that included the present states of Sinaloa, Nayarit, Jalisco, Colima and Michoacán, as well as parts of Guerrero and Guanajuato. Although groups of this region had basic features of Mesoamerican culture, in early times they developed a special tradition of their own known archaeologically from the shaft and chamber tombs. This special mortuary complex, including the ceramic offerings that accompanied the dead, suggest ties with South America. After A.D. 600 West Mexico gradually joined the

Burial No. 1 found in Chupícuaro, Guanajuato.

Mesoamerican world and was fully integrated with its culture by Postclassic times.

A general description will be made of some of the cultural features found in West Mexico throughout the different periods.

EARLY PRECLASSIC

The first highly developed cultures of this region are those of El Opeño in Michoacán (1500 B.C.), and the Capacha complex of Colima and Jalisco (1450 B.C.). Both of these cultures used advanced techniques to produce pottery of excellent quality. The oldest shaft tombs of which we have knowledge were found at El Opeño and were the prototype for those occurring in the following period.

LATE PRECLASSIC

Two important cultures derived from the Capacha-El Opeño tradition: that of Chupícuaro, Guanajuato, and the shaft tomb complex of Colima, Jalisco and Nayarit. Both cultures demonstrate a particular concern with funerary rites. The shaft tombs are composed of one or several underground chambers with entry from the surface through a vertical shaft. Here the dead were buried together with sumptuous offerings that included outstanding clay vessels and effigy figures.

CLASSIC

This was the high point of the shaft tomb period. The best pottery was produced, including effigy figures representing persons, plants and animals. Around 600 A.D. construction of the shaft tombs ceased and elements began to appear that show an affinity with the Mesoamerican world.

EARLY POSTCLASSIC

In this period a distinctive feature of Sinaloa and Nayarit is the Aztatlan complex, which is a manifestation of the artistic style of central Mexico known as the Mixteca-Puebla. Contact between the West and Central Mexico at this time is reflected in many of the arts, such as pottery, architecture and sculpture.

LATE POSTCLASSIC

The Tarascan people were prominent in this period, with their capital located at Tzintzuntzan on Lake Pátzcuaro. Like the Aztecs, the Tarascans became strong and powerful by conquest of an extensive area and collection of tribute from its inhabitants.

CULT OF THE DEAD

Chupícuaro is outstanding for the diversity of elaborate pottery vessels that were placed in the graves with the dead. The photograph shows the positioning of the bodies and offerings found in one of them. The vessels are highly varied in both shape and in decoration, the latter always made with geometric motifs.

The graves at Chupícuaro also contained figurines of various types. The female figurine in the photograph represents the one known as H-4 in which the long slanting eyes and ornaments are formed by applying small pieces of clay onto the flat body. It should be noted that while the figurines are generally naked, an elaborate headdress, necklace and earplugs are never lacking.

ARCHITECTURE

There are no remains of constructions from the early period in West Mexico, and our knowledge about them is limited to small clay models of temples and houses.

The example shown here is from Nayarit and demonstrates the activities of a family inside their house, a scene full of life and bustle. The polychrome decoration is typical of Nayarit and the designs are similar to those still made by the present-day Huichol Indians.

POTTERY

In addition to the solid figurines, beautiful hollow figures are also found in the shaft tombs. Those from Colima are red or black in color and highly polished. Most of them have spouts and therefore could have served as containers for liquids. They represent a variety of animals, realistically modeled, lifelike, and charming. Parrots are a common theme, such as the one we see here.

Silver washed *copper mask* of the God Xipe Totec. From Michoacán.

The hollow figures from Jalisco combine fine modeling with painting, usually in two colors. Most of them are anthropomorphic and are characterized by tall narrow heads and long thin noses, the eyes and nails carefully modeled. Representations of warriors are common in Jalisco, such as the one shown here. He is protected by armor and a helmet, and is shown in position for attack.

The hollow figures found in shaft tombs of Nayarit generally use several colors for indication of clothing, ornaments, and face and body paint. Here the predominant subject is human beings, nearly always adorned with ear and noseplugs made of multiple rings. Some are caricatures, and others are full of dignity, like the one illustrated.

STONE SCULPTURE

Near Mezcala, Guerrero, in the Río Balsas basin, many objects were carved of stone, some of them clearly showing Teotihuacán or Olmec influence. In this region they produced masks, axes in the shape of human figures, models of temples and various ornaments. The mask displayed here is in

the Mezcala style, which shows only the essential elements using schematic and sober lines.

THE AZTATLAN COMPLEX

In the Early Postclassic Sinaloa is distinguished by the Aztatlan complex, which includes vessels made of *tecali* (Mexican onyx), pottery masks, pipes and polychrome ceramics. The jar illustrated belongs to this complex, an example of the style known as Mixteca-Puebla or Cholulteca, which was widely distributed in Mesoamerica during the Postclassic period.

THE TARASCANS

The Tarascan culture is well known for its work in metal, producing both practical tools as well as jewelry. Here we see some tweezers that the priests hung around their necks as symbols of office and also used to remove facial hair. The other photograph shows a mask of the god Xipe Totec made of silver washed copper, beautifully executed and remarkably expressive.

PLAN OF UPPER FLOOR

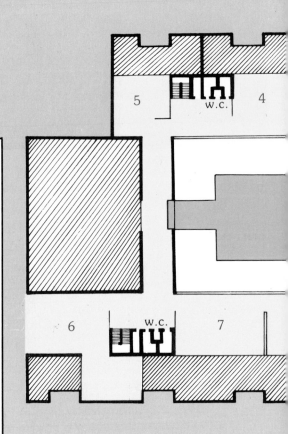

PLAN OF UPPER FLOOR

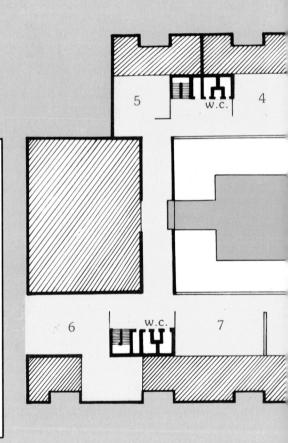

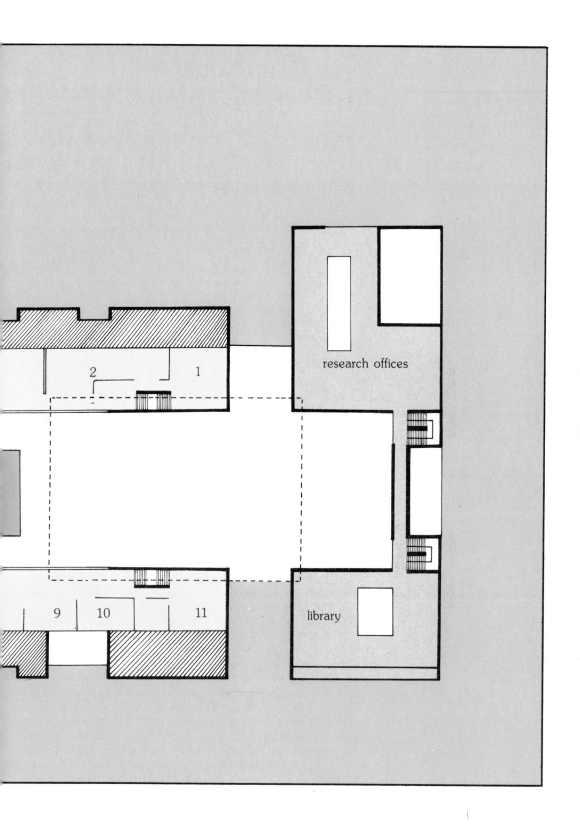

research offices

library

2   1

9   10   11

1. INTRODUCTION TO ETHNOGRAPHY

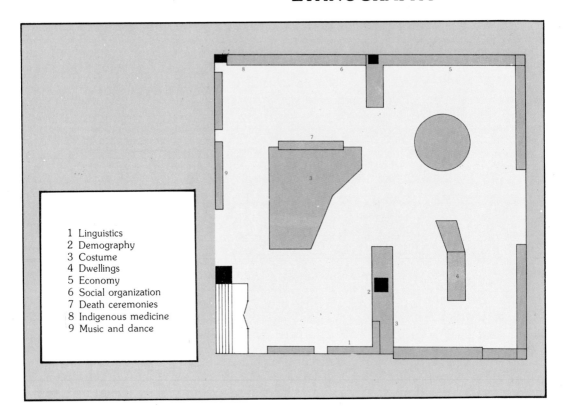

1 Linguistics
2 Demography
3 Costume
4 Dwellings
5 Economy
6 Social organization
7 Death ceremonies
8 Indigenous medicine
9 Music and dance

There are more than 3 million indigenous peoples speaking 56 different languages in present day Mexico. These are classified in four large groups: Joca-meridionals, Oto-mangue, Nahua-Cuitlateco and Maya-Totonaco.

These indigenous groups are mainly located in what was the great cultural area known as Mesoamerica where all the great pre-hispanic cultures were to be found.

With the European conquest in the XVI century, the indigenous population was subjected to a new socio-economic structure, which also contributed to resolve to a great extent, the problems facing the conquerors. This was to the detriment of the native population who, at the same time, also suffered a constant series of epidemics that diminished the population considerably throughout four centuries.

In the present century, the different ethnic groups are suffering an accelerated process of change. The young men and a large section of the economically active population, emigrate to the big cities with a view to improve their economic situation. In order to fill unqualified jobs, they need to understand Spanish and consequently abandon their mother tongue. The change is even more noticeable in their distinctive traditional costume which is left behind.

SETTLEMENT PATTERNS

Distribution of dwellings and agricultural lands are determined by the geography of the place. Therefore we find three types of settlements:

a) *Congregated*, when there is a definite plan and the houses are built next to each other.

b) *Semi-congregated*, when the houses are alternated with cultivated pieces of land and,

c) *Scattered*, when, because of the terrain, the dwellings are found scattered, perhaps in the cultivated areas. The different building materials vary according to the sorrounding environment. Generally the houses are rectangular, although there are exceptions such as the round houses with conical roofs found in the Huastec region and in other coastal communities of "adobe" or "bajareque" (sticks and wattle) and in some cases closely packed organ cactus, like the window-

In the XVIth century, after the Spanish conquest, many of the exquisite male adornments and garments such as the *tilma* and the *máxtlatl* disappeared, however the female garments such as the *huipil* and the *quechquémitl* survived.

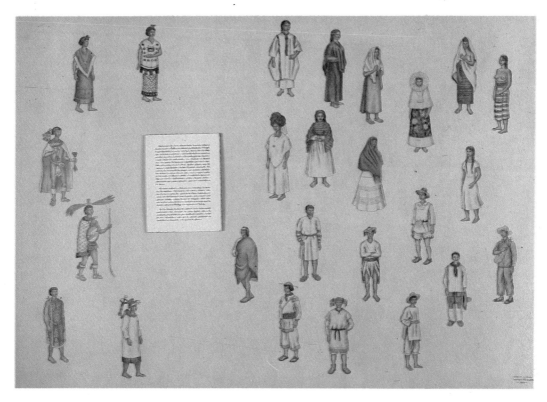

There are 56 indigenous groups living in Mexican territory at the present time. This *map* shows the different economic activities in which they are involved.

less dwellings of the kitchen, granery, ("temazcal") steam bath, corral and well.

ECONOMY

The most important products cultivated for home consumption are maize, beans, chile and pumpkin, although some groups are also involved in the commercial agriculture of coffee, sugar-cane, ornamental plants, fruits and flowers. In many of the indigenous regions, agricultural techniques are still similar to those of prehispanic times; in others, animal-drawn plows have been introduced, but there are very few who have adopted modern methods. This is because the steep slopes of the terrain and the eroded soil producing poor haversts does not permit modern technology.

ARTS AND CRAFTS

The manufacture of arts and crafts has been an important supplement in the indigenous economy of recent years. In fact, in several cases, it is the only source of income, such as in the villages making pottery using ancient manufacturing techniques. Every member of the family intervened in the handcraft and in some cases, the family workshop was enriched by other elements coming from outside the family craft. However, many of the old craftsmen are disappearing through lack of raw materials and an internal market. Furthermore, unfortunately, many of the indigenous objects such as jewelry and toys are being substituted by plastic products.

COMMERCE

The commercialization of agricultural and handcraft products usually took place at the weekly market *tianguis*, but in recent years, intermediaries have supplied money to the farmer or craftsman to buy his raw materials, thus obliging them to sell their agricultural produce or handcrafts at very low prices.

Each ethnic group stores its grain in *granaries* made of materials found in the surrounding area.

TRADITIONAL COSTUMES

One of the most characteristic features of the indigenous groups is their form of dress particularly emphasizing the woven fabrics.

Since prehispanic times, "the art of weaving" is an essential part of indigenous life in which both men and women are involved. The men shear the sheep for the wool, plant and harvest the cotton, prepare the dye and manufacture the different parts of the waist loom. The women spin, warp and weave on that marvellous loom that has been used ever since prehispanic times; they repeat old forms and designs, but also create new ones. The men proudly wear the overgarments, blankets, printed cottons and "mangas" which they make from natural fibers and which protect him from the cold and identify him as the bearer of a culture, as well.

Modern life has significantly affected the weavers' work: synthetic fabrics have replaced wool and cotton; commercial pigments have substituted natural dyes such as scarlet and snail colorants; magazine models have taken the place of the traditional designs, full of symbolism, and the original garments have made way for the modern dress.

The Spanish conquest established the rulings so as to the way that native women should dress; those who only wrapped themselves in a cloth and wore a *quechquémitl*, must wear a blouse, mainly for moral reasons. The men's apparel also changed rapidly, the "tilma" or knot fastened cloak, and the *máxtlat*, kind of loin cloth, were replaced by the cotton shirt and cotton breeches which in turn are fast disappearing now. The hat was adopted later and although leather thonged sandals are still worn, the materials used now have degen erated to tyre soles and plastic uppers.

In general, the women have shown less tendency to change as the *huipil* is still used in many places together with the long belt that holds it up. However, these are now combined with a blouse and shawl of definite Spanish influence.

CEREMONIES TO THE DEAD

All Souls Day and All Saints Day are particularly important festival days in Mexico. It is a time when the souls of the dead are venerated and offerings are made to them. These customs have given rise to ceremonies and rites that imply a traditional behavior controlling the community and its individuals, reinforcing family ties, relatives and friends. Nearing the month of November, the fields are filled with *cempoalxúchitl* (marigolds) proclaiming that everything should be prepared to receive the dead, the food should be prepared, the offerings, the candles and the flowers.

At the *tianguis* and market places, death transforms itself until it becomes a toy, a piece of bread, a candy and multiple

Following page. In order to make the *female indigenous costume*, the first process is to clean the fibres such as cotton and wool.

objects with which Mexicans joyfully have fun, turning a tragic event into a merry one.

Every region of Mexico has its particular way of celebrating and making their offerings to their dead. In the indigenous communities, the offerings are placed on family altars in the houses and they visit their dead in the local cemetery where they also place flowers or food on their graves.

The offering is the culmination of a cycle which starts with the death of an individual and continues with ceremonies related to the burial and others, such as the "carrying of the cross" which in many villages, is performed on the eighth or ninth day after death.

Certain elements are present in all the offerings such as objects and food that the dead person appreciated in his life and may include toys, clothing, work tools and musical instruments.

We can conclude by saying that the November festivities manifest the life-death duality that has been forever linked with the Mexican reality since prehispanic times.

POLITICAL AND RELIGIOUS ORGANIZATION

Many of the indigenous groups of Mexico still preserve their own ways of government and traditional religious organization which differ from the rest of the Mexican population certainly in these aspects.

The political organization links both the national and communal structures in such a way that it is the municipality which is the institution that overlays the local indigenous government. The municipality is formed by a group of public officials which include the municipality president, two main aldermen, two substitute aldermen and a trustee. In some villages the municipal president has a command stick and other symbols of power. His authority is only overruled by the principals or by the Council of the Elders which are indigenous institutions that still exist.

In some instances the political and religious organization intermingle in such a way, that the men have to pass through a series of offices during their life time, starting in the lowest rung of the hierarchial pyramid. The "topiles" fulfill various tasks that make them more aware of the way the organization functions. According to their performance, they may ascend the ladder from district attorney to majordomo. The latter is elected every year and his chief obligation is to pay for the fiesta of the community's Patron Saint, In some of these communities the civil and religious authorities dress specially for these particular occasions.

INDIGENOUS MEDICINE

Every region of Mexico has its
own particular way of placing
offerings to celebrate the dead.

In prehispanic times it was thought what sickness was
caused by the gods, by the influence of the calendar signs
on the day of the birth, by witchcraft or by natural causes.
Witchcraft was performed by *tlatlacatecolos* who had been
endowed at birth with their special powers under the precise
sign of the *tonalpohualli*. These specialists had a wide
knowledge of plants, minerals and animals with curative
properties. They also used the hallucinary methods produced
by mushrooms and "virgin seed" amongst other things.

In the same way, they knew incantation rites, ceremonies
and how to involve the spirits and divinities who had caused
the illnesses.

The Spanish colonizers brought with them the concepts
and practices of popular Spanish medicine. During the colonial
period when the Spaniards were consolidating their position, they imported slave labor from Africa, essential for the

137

colonial exploitation system. These ethnic groups also brought with them their own medicinal practices and these concepts, integrated with, what some people have called "mestizo" (mixed) medicine. It is thought that the origins of this mixed medicine can be found in the similarities and applications of indigenous, Spanish and African medicine.

In the present day, indigenous groups in Mexico have a profound knowledge of the plants, animals and minerals which are used in various methods to cure illnesses. They also make use of hallucinary plants such as mushrooms, peyote, virgin seed and so forth. These are considered sacred and are only eaten as part of a rite that only the healers and medicine men known.

The cause of the illness determines the type of cure according to the concepts held by the particular ethnic group. These causes may have been an offense against the gods of nature and the winds, ("chanes" or "chaneques") vapors from the dead, the evil eye, a severe fall or fright, eating cold or hot food or witchcraft.

Each group uses their own particular methods to find the cause, such as certain positioning of maize grains, holding eggs over the sick person, interpretation of dreams by the way in which the bark of a tree burns, or through helpful spirits, or consulting medicine books, feeling the pulse and sometimes even reading the cards.

The are all kinds of healers, some who are masseurs, quiropracticers, midwives, herbalists, those who use suction methods, those who cast spells, and medicine men. But only some of them know the accompanying rituals and ceremonies necessary to cure the patient. Sometimes herbs are used to extract the bad vapors or eggs to suck up the strange thing affecting the body. Besides prayers and rituals, they also use mineral dust or animals.

MUSIC AND DANCE

There is a great music and dance tradition within the Mexican ethnic groups, which originated in the late prehispanic period. These expressions were enriched by later introductions from Europeans and negros during the colonial period.

There were innumerable religious and military festivals in ancient Mexico that were always accompanied by music and singing. The indigenous people still honor their ancient gods with dances even though they may have adquired a

Catholic name. The Flyers Dance, the Acatlaxquis, the Huahuas, the Tlacololeros and the Dear Dance are all of prehispanic origin.

Prehispanic musical instruments still exist and include the *huéhuetl* (drum), *teponaztli*, rattles made of hollow pumpkins filled with little stones, the bone *chicahuaztli* with transverse incisions, earthenware or reed flutes and the *tenavaris*. To these were added the guitar, violin, harp, marimba and a small typical country guitar.

Prehispanic dances still survive such as *The Flyers*, typical of central Veracruz.

2. CORA HUICHOL

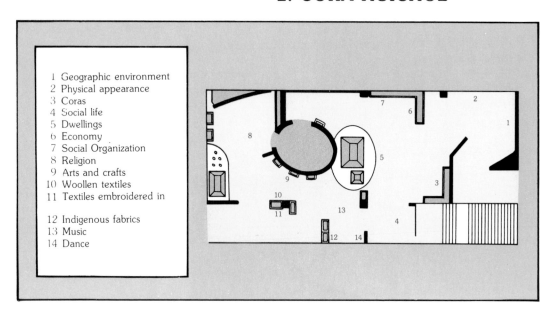

In this Hall, we have tried to show some of the most essential features of the Cora and Huichol indigenous groups which are among the least known and most isolated of Mexico.

GEOGRAPHIC CLIMATE

Both the Coras and Huicholes inhabit a geographic terrain of enormous mountains, deep ravines, rugged precipices and cliffs, small valleys and plateaus. All year round, numerous streams flow into the rivers running from north to south, which in the rainy season, swell to such proportions that they are impossible to cross. There is rich vegetation in the area particularly in timber yielding trees such as oak, "guanacaxtle" (*Enterolobium cyclocarpum*), mahogany, "chicozapote" (*Zapota achras*) red cedar, etc. There are also some fruit trees such as avocado, peach, guava, etc. The fauna of the region include deer, iguana and wild boar.

The climate in the low regions and the river valleys is hot, sometimes in the extreme, but in the higher regions, it varies from temperature to cold.

GEOGRAPHICAL SITUATION

The Cora and Huichol regions are found in the western Sierra Madre where the present states of Jalisco, Nayarit, Durango and Zacatecas join. The first area is in the Nayarit mountain range in the north of the state and the second is to the east of this in the north of Jalisco.

PHYSICAL APPEARANCE

The Coras are generally medium height, with beardless, fine featured faces. They have a strong personality, somewhat quarrelsome and are fighters. They have a manly appearance with an indomitable and independant spirit, fighting for their freedom. They were adept merchants, inclined to sell products such as "mezcal", various fibers and cloth, and the resale of salt and cattle, to the mixed races.

The Huicholes are more or less short and dark skinned with thick straight hair. They have prominent cheek bones with hardly any beard and no bodily hair. They are very strong physically, with an agreeable personality, generous, under-

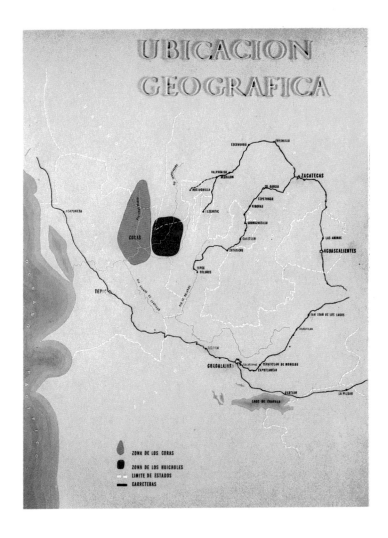

The Cora communities (orange) are found in Nayarit, *the Huicholes* (red) in Jalisco, both on the borders of Durango and Zacatecas States.

141

standing and hospitable. They have a good sense of humor which makes them laugh contagiously when they are together. Anything that confuses or causes ridicule or embarrassment to his neighbors is reason for laughter. This often causes bad tempers but they are immediately contented.

LANGUAGE

From the linguistic point of view, both the Cora and Huichol belong to the pima-cora familiy from yuto-nahua roots. Each group is comprised of a population of about 10,000 people and half of the Coras were registered bi-lingual in the 1970 census. However, in the same census it was found that more than 80% of the Huicholes were illiterate and about 60% spoke only their own language. There are scattered hamlets of Huicholes in the states of Nayarit, Durango and Zacatecas but the majority live in Jalisco.

HISTORY

Many researchers believe that both the Coras and Huicholes descend from groups coming from the northwest.

The Coras resisted the conquest from the moment they first made contact with Francisco Cortés de Buenaventura's European troops in 1524. Later between 1530 and 1531 under Nuño de Guzmán, they never let the Spanish army cross into the sierra and also rejected christian conversion.

The Coras and Huicholes, isolated in their mountains, retained their independence for centuries after the fall of Tenochtitlán. They were finally overcome in 1722 but they have offered fierce resistance to christianity and to any outside and foreign change. This has been their consistant characteristic attitude for a long time, clinging to their own cultural values, withstanding outside influence and maintaining, in a large measure, their own traditional culture.

The most colorful of the *indigenous costumes* is that of the Huicholes. There are mythical symbols in the embroidery which are entreaties.

CORAS

Some of the most outstanding examples of the Cora culture are exhibited in the display-case. Amongst the most conspicuous are the zoomorphic masks made from cactus fibers and paper and painted with earth colors and chemical paints. There are used in the Judea dance during Holy Week when many pagan and Christian rites are mixed, particularly surviving rites concerned with the biological phases of man which serve to integrate him into the society. At the beginning of the passion drama on the Thursday night, the Judea dancers dressed only in a loin cloth with their bodies painted in colored stripes, dance round the village square. As they dance with their heads down, gesticulating, they represent the spirits of Spring who promote the fruitful growth of plants and animals. Following this, they perform the magic turtle dance, which is a sexual symbolism ritual, or a puberty iniciation rite which expresses the desire to preserve the species and assure the fertility of the earth and agricultural produce. (It is said that, when there are no women present, they remove their loin-cloths.)

HOUSING

The building materials for both the Cora and Huichol dwellings, are provided by the surrounding environment, according to the climate. The Huicholes live in one rectangular shaped room with a dirt floor, no windows and an opening for an entrance. They have two or four sloping roofs made of straw. There are differences in the Cora houses, since many of them have tiled roofs with an open corridor made of wood particularly in Santa Teresa. In both cases, the room serves as sleeping quarters, kitchen and storage, although in many cases, the kitchen is built separately together with other additions such as the granary built on pilons. The latter is called a cart of "chipil" by the Coras and has a straw roof. When it is not used to store maize, it is used as a temporary dormitory.

SETTLEMENT PATTERN

Due to the rugged terrain, the settlements are distributed throughout the sierra in small hamlets concentrated round the ceremonial centers which act as political-religious and administrative focal points. Here, there are only a few uninhabited huts belonging to the chiefs who only use them when assemblies are called, or civic or religious functions pertaining to the community are celebrated. Only a few people who perform some ceremonial office live there. These festivals are gatherings and serve to promote harmony and social cohesion among the community members. The Cora

ceremonial centers are found in Jesus María, Mesa de Ñayar, Santa Teresa, San Francisco, Saycota, Rosarito, San Pedro Ixcatan and San Juan Corapan. Those of the Huicholes are found in San Andrés Cohamiata, Santa Catarina Coexcomatitlán, San Sebastián Teponahuastlán, Guadalupe Ocotán and Tuxpan de Bolaños.

Generally the Huichole dwelling consists of only one room without windows which serves as both sleeping quarters, kitchen and storeroom. There is a thatched roof over wattle walls and a dirt floor.

SOCIAL ORGANIZATION

There are civilian authorities within each of these communities under which jurisdiction falls the upkeeping of social order, they are: a governor, a judge or mayor, a captain, a constable and several "topiles" (minor functionaries). They also have their own religious authorities who watch over and direct all that is related to the deities and their cult. In the religious hierarchy, the warden and his assistants for each saint stand out, besides the *mara'akáme,* to whom they attribute supernatural powers and the role of being a mediator between deities and man.

The Huicholes observe a strict group intermarrying and whoever marries outside of it faces the risk of losing his identity and is labeled as a danger to the group unity.

ECONOMY

The economy is based on the cultivation of maize, beans and pumpkins grown in communal lands dependent on seasonal rains. The soil is thin and rough where the plots of land are and as a consequence, production is extremely poor. Moreover, many of them are on steep stony slopes needing laborious clearing with primitive hoes and wooden planting sticks. On the few pieces of land that can be plowed, they use wooden plows and rakes pulled by oxen.

This economy is supplemented with hunting, fishing and gathering which complement their diet. Also some members sell their arts and crafts and many hire themselves out as labor force to work in the tobacco plantations, cutting sugarcane or other agricultural labor needed on the Nayarit coast.

RELIGION

The present day Huichol religion is very much a mixture of prehispanic and catholic elements in which the traditional religious practices hold greater sway. These practice are based on a rich store of myths and in the sacred chants that gave birth to a large pantheon of gods who govern the greatest heavenly bodies, the lowest animal, or the most minute detail of a natural phenomenum. The Huichol reverts to myth and magic to satisfy his need to understand phenomena. For the Huichol, his ancestors were transformed into divine spirits and creators with a human resemblance. After making penance, they would die, going through many processes of disembodiment and scattering their limbs to permit the birth of the nourishing natural elements. That is to say, they offered plants, animals and fruits of the earth to man, which implies that the Huichol should correspond by making offerings to the gods. The word "god" does not exist in the Huichol world because the deities are known by ritual names of relatives such as *Tatehuari*, god of fire, Our Grandfather; *Tayau*, god of the sun, Our Father and so on. According to the occasion, they offer *niericas*, arrows, vessels, votive, tables, *muvieris, takuatzi*, god's eyes, small curved stools carved in stone or made of wicker, gourds, incense burners, *etcetera*.

PEYOTE

During the celebration of certain religious festivities, such as the agricultural cycle ceremonies, and in order to be in communion with the deities, the Huicholes eat *híkuri* or peyote *(Lophophora williamsü)*, a small cactus of a wide, flat

and boneless crown, which they consider sacred and with great therapeutical powers for the body as well as the mind. Peyote is a highly complex hallucinogenic plant due to the psychoactive substances it contains; over thirty alkaloids which behave differently from one another; some with sedative and soporific properties, while others increase the reflex excitability of the nervous system. Among the main alkaloids there are peyotine, lophophorine, and anhalonidine, all biodynamically active, but mescaline is the basic agent which induces visions, that not only include brightly colored images and gentle glowing auras which seem to surround all natural objects, but also induces hearing, tasting, smelling and tactile sensations, as well as those of weightlessness, sharpening vision with the naked eye and alterations in time and space perceptions.

Wool decorated boards and other votive objects depict mythic symbols and scenes which are petitions for good health, well-being, rain etcetera.

ARTS AND CRAFTS

Anything related to the domestic production of clothing and arts and crafts is particularly outstanding in this ethnic group. Their embroidery and woven fabrics where various techniques, designs and colors are employed are specially noteworthy and there is also a considerable amount of glass bead work produced by the men.

3. TARASCANS, PUREPECHAS

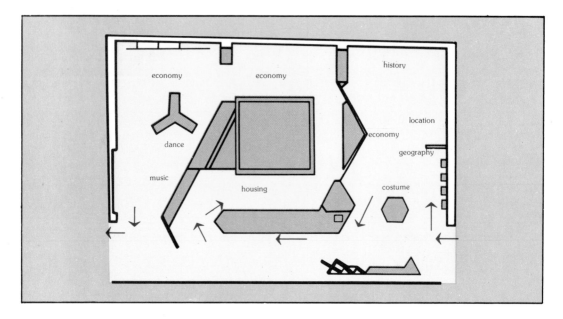

The Tarascans or Purépechas live in the Tarasca Plateau in the state of Michoacán.

There are two versions of the origin of the name Tarasca. One is that there was a god called "Taras" from whom the name derived and the other was derived from the term *tarhascue*, which the indigenous used to define the father-in-law or son-in-law of Spaniards married to indigenous women and it was the Spaniards who called them Tarascans.

The Tarascan population is now distributed in three regions, in the sierra, in the ravine and in the lakes. The greatest number of Purépecha communities are found in the lake area of Pátzcuaro and the surrounding mountains with a smaller number in the ravines.

Insofar as the Tarascan language is concerned, linguistic studies have shown a very remote relationship with other Mesoamerican tongues, such as: Totonaca, Mixe and Mayan. It has also been noted that there is a distant link to the Zuñi in the U.S.A. and the Quechua in South America.

At the time of the Spanish conquest, the Tarascan state was a military technocracy sustained by an extensive military and secular tributary system governed by a supreme chief or *cazonci*.

The Mexicas sought, unsuccessfully, for an alliance with the Tarascans, to repel the Spaniards. Once the Mexican were conquered, Cortés ordered Cristóbal de Olid to take possession of Taximaroa in 1522, which fell without resistance from the last Tarascans governor, Tzinzicha Tangaxoan.

Later, once the colonial society was established and the indigenous society surrendered, the Spanish crown grouped together the scattered Tarascan population who were riddled with sickness. They congregated in monastery-hospitals where religious communities looked after the sick, orphans and the general needs of the indigenous. One of these hospitals was Santa Fe de la Laguna by Pátzcuaro lake, founded by the first bishop of Michoacán, Vasco de Quiroga. Deeply influenced by the utopian ideas of Thomas More, in 1565 Quiroga enacted a series of bylaws so as to define the nature of the Franciscan Hospitals, commending the friars, among some of their duties, that of teaching useful trades to the native indians, men and women alike.

HUNTING

One of the traditional prehispanic customs still preserved by the Tarascans today, was duck hunting, usually at the

The Purépechas still preserve a prehispanic custom of *hunting ducks* by throwing chaff and using harpoons. "Tamales" are made from the meat and are offerings for the dead.

end of October. *Corundas variches*, which are a kind of tamale were made of duck meat and used in the festivities to the Dead on All Souls and All Saints Day. This activity is shown in the diorama where the type of harpoons *átlatl* and indigenous hunting gear used can be seen in the panel on the right.

CLOTHING

Little by little the men have abandoned their traditional costume and now wear industrially made clothes like most of the country folk, but in some of the lake and hill communities they still use rough cotton shirts and baggy pants with a woven belt, woollen blanket, leather-thong sandals and a hat.

The Tarascan women's garb varies according to the place. Some of the riverside communities of the sierra still wear skirts with a bright colored strip of material at the top and a similarly colored flounce on the bottom to protect them from the prickly ground. This skirt is made up of multiple folds joined to a waistband. It is called a roll and is held in place at the waist by a long girdle. The blouse or "guanengo" is made of rough cotton, either embroidered, or drawn-thread work at the neck and shoulders and tucked in at the waist. They also use navy blue shawls with either pale blue or white stripes.

AGRICULTURE

The fundamental economic activity of the Tarascan is agriculture, even in the areas where fishing is important, such as the lake region and especially on the islands. The main crops are maize, wheat, beans and pumpkins together with a little horticulture and vegetables.

FISHING

Fishing is another of the activities carried out by the inhabitants of the shores of lake Pátzcuaro. They use harpoons, traps and distinctive nets. The entire family is involved, as the women make the nets and the men and the youngsters go out on the lakes to fish. When there is plenty of fish, they sell the excess in the market.

DWELLINGS

Following page. Women living in the sierra use long pleated woollen skirts, a shawl and woven belt.

In the ravine and lake regions, the houses are made of stone and adobe (mud bricks) with tiled roofs but in the hills the houses are called "trojes" (barns) and are made of wood.

ECONOMIC ORGANIZATION

The vast quantity of raw materials available in the region since prehispanic times, allowed each Tarascan village to specialize in particular trades that exploited their resources.

METAL WORK

Plentiful amounts of copper made the Tarascans the first Mesoamerican people who most used metals for practical purposes. They still do beaten copper work although now for purely commercial reasons in Santa Clara del Cobre, now called Villa Escalante.

They also worked in gold and silver but now only silver is worked in Pátzcuaro, Chilchota and Cherán, where they manufacture the rosaries given to newly-weds. The only village that still works in gold is Huetamo.

Following page. Dance was closely associated to the religious festivals and often the dancers were fulfilling a promise to the Patron Saint of the village.

3. Indumentaria para la danza
de los Negritos. Uruapan.

Even though synthetic fibres have substituted woollen fabrics, some communities still weave their textiles on *pedal looms* such as this one.

OTHER INDUSTRIES

In the present day some of the arts and crafts have been substituted by industrial goods but there still exist villages who preserve their small industries to supplement their revenue with wood work, pottery and weaving.

WOODWORK

Among the woodwork that is found in the region, one finds the manufacture of chocolate whisks, flower vases, powder boxes, toys (such as whipping tops and cup-and-ball game), spoons and carved ladles.

It seems that tray and cup lacquer work is a handicraft practiced by the natives ever since the prehispanic era. The objects are covered with a semiliquid pulp, which is produced by mixing the grease of an insect called "axe" and the oils that are extracted from the "chía" and "chicalote" seeds, or linseed oil mixed with dolomitic powder. Afterwards, they are polished and painted through different techniques. This handicraft is prevalescent of Michoacán, mainly among some artisans from Uruapan, Pátzcuaro and Quiroga.

POTTERY

In the Tarasca Plateau, pottery has developed into an economic activity. There are clay mines in the hills that supply two or more villages which make ceramics. Such is the case of the Patamban deposit exploited by its own Patamban village and San José de Gracia, Cocuchucho and Ocumicho villages. There are many pottery workshops on the plateau in Tzintzuntzan, Santa Fé, Erongarícuaro, Patamban and other villages.

WEAVING

Woolen cloth is made in Nahuatzen, Santa Clara, Paracho, Pátzcuaro, Zacapu, Parangaricutiro and San José de las Colchas. Shawls and serviettes are made on waist looms in Aranza, using fine thread and a "gauze" technique. In Pichátaro and Uricho the serviettes are made of thicker cotton decorated with glassbead work in animal, flower and geometrical designs with a fringe on only one side. This work is known as "glass bead embroidery".

The festivals and everything related to them, form an essential part of the Tarascan live. Among the most important manifestations linked to the religious calendar are the passion plays and the dances.

4. THE OTOMIANS

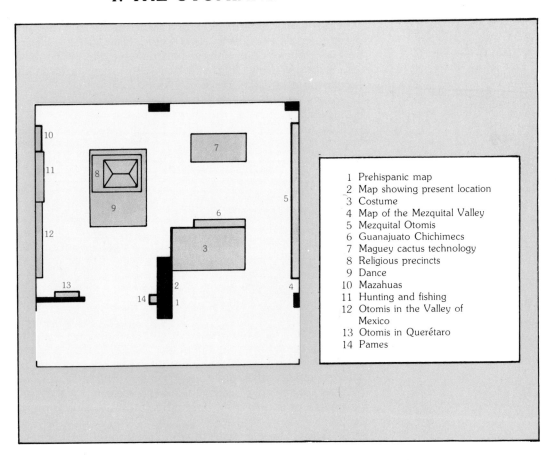

1 Prehispanic map
2 Map showing present location
3 Costume
4 Map of the Mezquital Valley
5 Mezquital Otomis
6 Guanajuato Chichimecs
7 Maguey cactus technology
8 Religious precincts
9 Dance
10 Mazahuas
11 Hunting and fishing
12 Otomis in the Valley of Mexico
13 Otomis in Querétaro
14 Pames

HISTORY

In the XVI century when the Spaniards arrived, the Otomians linguistic group occupied a large area in the Mexican upper plateau. Culturally they were divided in three opposing groups who formed part of agricultural Mesoamerican culture. These were the Otomí and Mazahua, Matlatzinca and Ocuilteca, whilst the Chichimecas in the north, were part of a hunting and gathering culture and the Pames, were a group with characteristics some where between the two.

LOCATION

At the present time, the Otomians live in Michoacán, Hidalgo, Puebla, Querétaro, Veracruz, San Luis Potosí, Tlaxcala and Guanajuato. They live on the outskirts of the towns or in the fields which tend to be scattered.

HOUSING AND FURNITURE

Their dwellings differ according to the climate and the building materials available in each region. Usually the walls are built of adobe or brick with red earthenware tiles on a gabled roof. The typical dwelling in the Mezquital Valley, is the smallest of them all and is built of rough stone and cactus leaf walls. There are additions such as a granary and an altar that may be inside, or outside, the dwelling place.

They have scant furnishing and usually use palm or tulle leaf mats placed on the floor to sleep. Their blankets are home made or locally manufactured.

CLOTHING

The traditional female costume is made of a simple dress or a piece of cloth wound round the waist held in place with a belt, a shirt or jacket, *quechquémitl* over blouse and shawl. Each woman, in every village, has her own way of wearing the clothes and uses her own decorative motifs.

The Temoayan Otomís in the State of Mexico use a woollen *huishu* made out of four pieces of cloth joined together with a fine lace trimming, instead of a *quechquémitl* (overblouse). The Mazahua women of Temazcalzingo, also in the State of Mexico, embroider their *quechquémitl* profusely and the Otomís in the Mezquital Valley have double woven *quechquémitl* that give the appearance of being double-sided. The blouses are embroidered on the front and sleeves with floral, geometric or zoomorphic decorative motifs in one or many colors.

Only the older men wear the rough cotton shirts and pants, whilst most of the rest now wear manufactured clothes over which they use a woollen "gabán" and a straw hat.

THE HIDALGO OTOMIS

The Otomís in the state of Hidalgo mainly inhabit the Mezquital Valley which is a semi-desertic region bordered in the north by the Juárez sierra, in the south by the Mexe hills, with the Xuthe sierra in the west and in the east, the range of hills running from the Cerro del Fraile to the Cerro del Aguila and the Actopan sierra.

The Valley is irrigated by the Tula river whose main tributary is the San Juan river with its source in Querétaro. There are a few small streams such as the Alfajayucan and a series of thermal and sulphur springs which include Ajacuba, Vito, Tepé, Calera, Dios Padre and Tolantongo.

To help the water storage for agriculture, various reservoirs have been built in the present century, such as the Requena, Endo, Recodo and others. These have divided the Valley into two areas. The northern area which has an irrigation system of fifteen townships and the arrid area in the south with fourteen townships, where the greatest number of Otomí speaking inhabitants live.

ECONOMY

The land ownership problem is serious, since the inheritance system and the distribution of common lands has fragmented the land in such a way, that a small holding is not sufficient to maintain a familiy of five or more members. This causes the small holders to hire themselves out as day laborers or the working partner on their own lands, to those who have sufficient capital to rent and cultivate the land.

The main crop within the economic and ritual activities is maize. More than a third of the state of Hidalgo's agricultural production comes from the irrigated area where they plant alfalfa, maize, wheat, tomatoe and chile.

The Otomí in the arrid area, due to the poor yield of the land, exploits all the natural resources within his means to produce the arts and crafts that are made in the family group. Among crafts the moulded domestic pottery shows two well

The Otopame linguistic family formed by the Mazahua, Matlatzinca, Ocuilteca, Pame and Chichimec jonaz are found in the State of Mexico, Hidalgo, Michoacán, Puebla, Veracruz, Querétaro, San Luis Potosí and Tlaxcala.

The Otomís in the Mezquital Valley derive most of their economy from the *maguey* cactus. From this hardy plant, they obtain building material for their dwellings, fibres and food products.

defined characteristics. The first is of prehispanic tradition of single firing and sealed decoration, such as the type seen in the Chapantango jugs (pots). The second, show elements introduced in the colonial period and are double fired, such as the incense pots and earthenware cooking pots from Santiago Loma and San Pablo Oxtotilpan. Wicker work, weaving in "ixtle" vegetable fibers and palm leaves are also typical in the arrid zone.

The manufacture of textiles in the Mezquital region is still one of the most important productions. The men make heavy woollen "gabán" and blankets on the pedal looms and the women continue to work on their waist looms, producing *quechquémitl*, bags and shoulder bags with the traditional bird designs.

MAGUEY CACTUS TECHNOLOGY

A large part of the indigenous economy is provided by the maguey cactus. This plant is sufficiently strong to withstand the arrid and calcarus soil of the region. The Otomís have always used this plant to its maximum advantage since prehispanic times.

The much appreciated fiber called *ixtle* in Náhuatl and *santhé* in Otomí, is obtained from the agave plant by and age-old tradition. The Otomí man places the fleshy part of the plant on a plank and pressing down with his small, iron tipped, wood carving tool begins his work. He extracts the fleshy central part first, called *xixi* and scrapes until the fibers are cleaned. An eight hour day, represents the working of about 30 plants and then the "ixtle" is washed with maize water or soapy water to remove the acidity from the fiber. This is a necessary process so that the spinners hands are not damaged.

Once the fiber has been obtained, it must then be spun by either the Otomí men, women, elderly or children. This may be done when they are walking along the road, listening to mass, in the market, in the religious festivals, looking after their animals or even at a funeral wake. Once enough fiber has been spun, the women begin to weave the "ayate". Those "ayates" that are manufactured in the region range from the simplest type, used for agricultural tasks, to the very finest; the latter never to be used for commercial purposes, since it is a matter of great pride either to wear them, or to present them as gifts to the loved ones.

The "maguey" cactus also provides elements for house building as well as nourishing products.

SACRED SHRINES

The sacred shrines, called *tinik* in Otomí and *intimi* in Mazahua are situated in the dwellings, or out in the fields. Each shrine is dedicated to some catholic saint such as the Virgin Mary and the Chalma Christ being the most popular. These are represented by the usual images placed on an altar at the back of the shrine. Nearing the date of the Patron Saint of the shrine, it is decorated with garlands of fresh,

Among the Otomís, *dance* is a mixture of Prehispanic and Spanish customs and are performed fulfilling a promise made to the Patron Saint of the place.

159

or paper flowers, wooden crosses, incense burners, candles and a newly embroidered robe.

DANCE

Dance is a plastic expression fundamental to any group of people and among the Otomís, it reveals a distinctive mixture of prehispanic and Spanish customs that blend various features which differentiate them from the surrounding peoples. The only similarity with the neighboring people is that their dances are performed for similar reasons, in that they are promises to the Patron Saint of their home village. The dancer covers all his personal expenses and what is needed to make his costume.

THE ECONOMY OF THE MAZAHUAS

The Mazahuas inhabit the west of the State of Mexico where their agricultural economy is based on maize, complemented with the extraction of "zacatón", fodder grass roots for fiber. They also produce double-fired and high-temperature fired pottery and some silver work, in which the necklaces and earrings of animal and plant motifs are particularly outstanding. The women still weave their profusely embroidered *quechquémitl* on the waist looms. Wheat stalk weaving is also produced among the crafts of the region, very similar to that produced by the Tarascans.

OTOMIS IN THE STATE OF MEXICO

Although technological advances have done away with many of the lagoons that drained into the Otomí region of the State of Mexico, some of the indigenous people still fish the "acocil" (kind of fresh-water crayfish) in the rainy season. Tamales of little fish, baked carp and the "acocil" crustacean are sold in the markets to complement the basic diet of "tortillas", chile and beans. These fish are caught with of small hand nets.

The Otomís of the State of Mexico are famous for their weaving, particularly their "ixtle" bags such as those displayed in the show case. They also work bone and horn, producing items such as combs, earrings, bracelets, broaches and chess sets, which are not only sold in the Toluca market but also in fairs throughout the Republic.

MEDICINE

To this day, many indigenous people still use curative methods dating from prehispanic times. These methods overcame the methods introduced by the conquerors because the pharmacutical properties available in the Mesoamerican

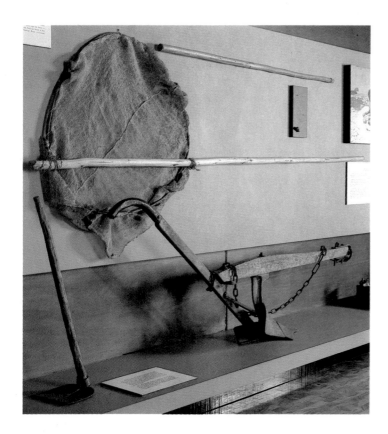

The Otomís in the **Toluca**-Ixtlahuaca Valley use *bag nets* for catching freshwater shrimps. Their agricultural instruments such as the hoe and plow are made of wood.

herbs were already well established. They are now labelled as analgesics, diuretics, ocotics and narcotics.

Today, as long ago, the indigenous healer is indoctrinated with supernatural knowledge. For the indigenous people, illness is not merely an organic disorder, but also evidence of the untrammelled wrath of the gods or ancestors. The physical disorder may have been caused partly by eating cold or hot foods, or fresh or heavy foods.

The hallucinary or "heavenly" mushrooms are frequently used among the Matlatzinca healers. These are considered sacred because of all the extraordinary experiences that they provoke. The mushrooms are eaten raw, whithout cleaning, in multiples of five after being smoked and are accompanied with sugar or fruit. The healer and his patient eat the mushrooms at the same time to diagnose the illness and suggest the right sort of medicine to be used in the treatment.

5. THE NORTH PUEBLA SIERRA

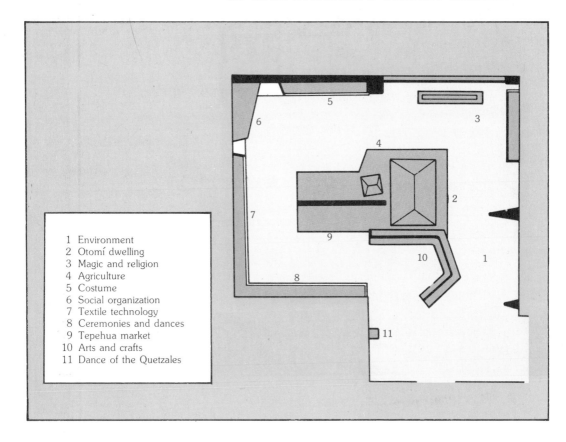

1 Environment
2 Otomí dwelling
3 Magic and religion
4 Agriculture
5 Costume
6 Social organization
7 Textile technology
8 Ceremonies and dances
9 Tepehua market
10 Arts and crafts
11 Dance of the Quetzales

During the prehispanic period the North Puebla Sierra belonged to Totonacapan, which was part of the Cempoala kingdom and was incorporated into the Mexica empire with the conquests of Tizoc and Ahuizotl. Numerous groups of Nahuas coming from two cultural backgrounds, emmigrated to this region in the XVth century. There were those speaking náhuatl languages coming from the Central Upper Plains who settled round Huauchinango and Zacatlán, and those coming from the center and south of the state of Puebla, also Náhuatl speaking, who seattled in Teziutlán, Tlatlauqui, Zacapoaxtla and Cuetzalan. This was how Nahuas came to settle in Totonaca territory.

ECOLOGY

Following page. The Otomí women of San Pablito still preserve the beautiful traditional designs of their native costume.

The North Puebla Sierra forms part of the Eastern Sierra Madre which starts at the junction of the Ocotepec and Libres townships. From there, it opens out to the east and west

and includes Chignahuapan, Zacatlán and Tulancingo, as far as Teziutlán and Tlapacoya. In the northeast, the terrain changes to gentle hills until it reaches the Gulf coast of Mexico.

The vegetation includes conifers in the higher regions of this area, oak, eagle wood and madroña in the temperate climate and the lichen parasitic plants of tropical forests. Unfortunately, the immoderate felling of trees has endangered the region and has deteriorated large areas of forests provoking serious soil erosion.

The most important rivers in the region are the Pantepec, Cazones and Necaxa which form plentiful waterfalls. Necaxa, one of the oldest hydroelectric plants supplying Mexico City, is found in this area.

Despite indiscriminate hunting which has caused the extinction of certain species such as the small ocelot and small deer, there is plenty of fauna which include armadillos, badgers, rodents, reptiles and beutifully feathered birds.

This region of the north Sierra, is impressive for its beautiful vegetation, always green and humid and inhabited by many peoples: the Nahuas or Mexicans, the Totonacs, the Tepehuas and the Otomís.

AGRICULTURE AND LIVESTOCK

The most important agriculture is the growing of maize, coffee, fruit trees and sugar cane. The indigenous people profit from the distribution and commercialization of the latter products which they control. A typical example of this is coffee, mainly grown by the indigenous people in Teziutlán, Xicotepec, Cuetzalan and Zihuateutla. They transport the whole grain and sell it to a middle man very cheaply. He processes it and sells it at a much higher price to the monopolizers or to a who are subject to variations of the international cofee market prices.

In latter years, the area has also commercialized the production of apples, oranges, lemons, avocados, potatoes and chile since the opening up of highways leading to commercial centers such as Huauchinango, Cuetzalan, Ahuacatlán, Xicotepec and Teziutlán. Even so, in many parts of the Sierra, transportation is still by foot or horseback and therefore mule driving is still important.

Sugar cane is cultivated in the northwest of the region and is made into unrefined brown sugar and the "refino" is an alcoholic beverage of the Sierra. The Huauchinango municipality includes villages which now cultivate ornamental plants that are marketed mainly in Monterrey, Guadalajara and Mexico City.

Cattle raising is also carried out in Xicotepec de Juárez, Zacapoaxtla and Teziutlán but is mainly in the hands of the "mestizos" who have large cattle ranches. An agricultural

fair is organized every year from the 9th of July to the 6th of August in Teziutlán.

In this Otomí dwelling we can observe the domestic utensils used for cooking.

HUNTING AND GATHERING

The indigenous people of the area hunt "tlacuaches" (kind of opossum), armadillos and birds. They also catch fresh water cray fish "acamaya". They collect blackberries "quelites", wild vegetable plants, "yuca" and herbs. These all form part of their diet and are sold in the weekly markets.

COMMERCE

The Nahuas go to the markets in Zacapoaxtla, Huauchinango, Cuetzalan, Ahuacatlán, Teziutlán and Zacatlán whilst the Totonacs use Xicotepec and Papantla, the Otomís go to Tenango de Doria and Pahuatlán and the Tepehuas to Mecapalapa, Huauchinango and Villa Juárez.

DWELLINGS

These dwellings consist of a rectangular room with a double sloping roof. The construction materials depend on the geographic zone and the economic situation of the inhabitants. Therefore, sometimes we find "adobe" houses with thatched roofs or wooden slat or reed houses with thatched roofs. Otomí dwellings have lofts where they store working tools and seeds. Generally the granaries are built of logs next to the dwellings.

TEMAZCAL

The *temazcal* is situated in the yard of the house. This is a kind of steam bath of prehispanic origin that is still in use, despite the fact that when the friars noticed its profound religious significance, they tried to suppress it. Today, there is still talk of the Lord or Lady of the *temazcal* and they still place a cross, a wooden arch, or flowers at the door.

BARK PAPER ("AMATE")

The Otomís from the village of San Pablito, Pahuatlán in the state of Puebla make a kind of paper from the bark of a tree for magic-religious purposes. They still venerate the Sun, Water, Fire and Earth in this place and still render homage to the cult of the "Spirits" and the "Lord Protectors". The healers cut out figures of the "Lords" and "Spirits" from the bark paper to pay homage in the cults and ceremo-

Bark fibres are placed on a plank to hammer them into *bark paper*.

166

Nahua women card and wind wool to begin the long process of making belts and girdles.

nies called "el costumbre" (the tradition) which take place in the hills, caves and fountains where they live.

One of the most important ceremonies is the baptizing of the seeds which takes place every year in the maize fields, to assure a good harvest. These bark paper figures of the "Spirits" and "Lords" are also used in the curing rites for illnesses caused by frights or bad vapors.

They still use prehispanic techniques to cure the bark paper. The bark is cut off a "jonote" (*Helicarpus americanus*) tree and put to boil in a copper pot with water and ashes for about four to six hours. Then it is taken out and dried, after which, the fibers are placed one by one on a board, forming a square. These are beaten with a stone beater until the fibers join together to make a paper surface.

In 1950 the Nahuas of Guerrero started to paint these bark papers and immediately created a successful national and international market. This then became the principal industry of the San Pablito community, in which the men, women and children were all involved. Therefore, bark paper manufacturing stopped being an exclusive activity of the healers.

COSTUME

The costume in the Northern Sierra of Puebla is very colorful: the women wear blouses, sashes, wrap-arounds, *quechquémitl* and shawls. These garments have such particular characteristics in their materials, techniques, colors and designs, that it makes it easy for them to tell the difference between the Nahuas, Totonacas, Tepehuas and Otomíes.

For example, the *quechquémitl* worn by the Totonacas and Tepehuas is made either of cotton or wool, woven on the waist loom using a particular brocade technique in bright colors. The *quechquémitl* of the Nahuas in Coacuila, Cuetzalan and Atla, is made of cotton and is tailored through a gauze technique; those which show drawings of beautifully stylized animals do stand out. The Otomí women wear one made of cotton and wool, embroidered with traditional colors and designs; the lower border of this *quechquémitl* has a strip made with a curved weaving process, unique in Mexico.

The Otomí *quechquémitl* has a purple stripe woven in a curve, unique in Mexico.

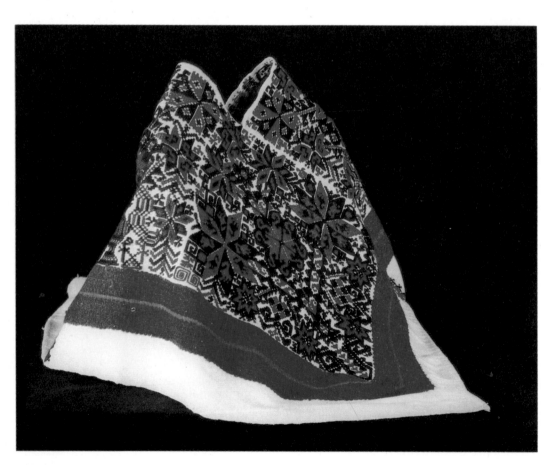

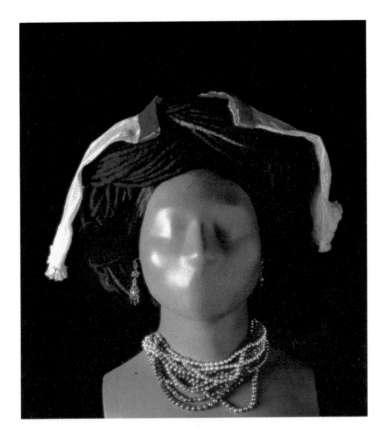

The women's square-collared blouses differ only in the embroidering, which may either be hand-made or, as in the case of the Chachahuantla women, machine made.

The wrap-around may be made either of cotton or wool. The Tepehua women trim it with machine embroidery in its lower border.

The most outstanding sashes are those worn by the Tepehua women; they are blue and have a double weaving.

The Nahua women of Cuetzalan decorate their head with the *mastahual*, a headdress made of woolen strips, which they wind around their head in the shape of a crown.

In some of the villages of the Sierra, the waist loom is no longer in use. Cotton and wool have been replaced by synthetic fibers, hence the natives now use industrial fabrics to make their traditional costumes.

RELIGIOUS ORGANIZATION

The wardenship, an organization which allows the celebration of the yearly festivity cycle, is made up of the wardens and their "topiles" (minor functionaries) or "esquineros" (corner-men). Among the Tlaola Nahuas, the most impor-

The Totonacs and Tepehuas take products to *the market* that have taken many long hours of work to make.

Following page. The dance of the Quetzales performed in the indigenous festivals is famous for its impressive feathered headdress. It probably originally had an agricultural-astronomic significance.

tant change of wardenship takes place on August 24. The outgoing warden and his wife carry the religious images and staffs of command to the church, amidst music, incense and fireworks. The incoming wardens carry the offering, which consists of clay (earthenware) pots containing "tepache" (a fermented drink), chocolate and water, as well as bread baskets, candles and flowers. A Catholic priest celebrates Mass and, at the end, the healers purify the wardens with flowers and candles. When the ceremony is over, all people attending it, wearing necklaces and crowns made of *cempoalxúchitl* flower (marigolds), dance to the traditional *xochipitzahua* dance.

In the Northern Sierra of Puebla, the native dances always contain a strong religious character. The dancer fulfills a "promise" to the Patron Saint of the place to dance on his festival day if he has granted him a good harvest and good health. The night before the festival, offerings are prepared and prayers are said in which, the dancers are purified by the healers. The most well known dances are the dance of the Flyers, the Quetzales, Santiagos, Acatlaxquis and the Negritos.

6. OAXACA REGION

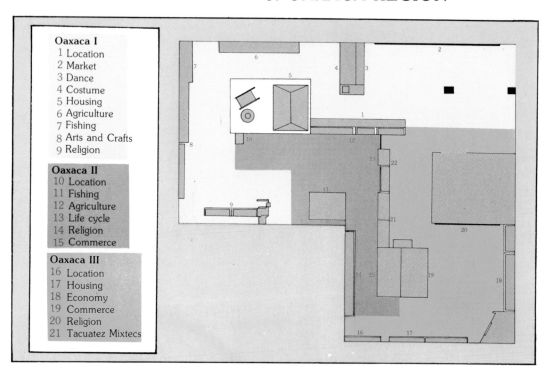

Oaxaca I
1 Location
2 Market
3 Dance
4 Costume
5 Housing
6 Agriculture
7 Fishing
8 Arts and Crafts
9 Religion

Oaxaca II
10 Location
11 Fishing
12 Agriculture
13 Life cycle
14 Religion
15 Commerce

Oaxaca III
16 Location
17 Housing
18 Economy
19 Commerce
20 Religion
21 Tacuatez Mixtecs

The state of Oaxaca situated in the south of the Mexican Republic is characterized by its extremely mountainous terrain where there are various climates within small areas containing fast flowing rivers. Due to the diverse climatic and geographical characteristic in the Isthmus region of Mexico, there are also a great variety of ethnical and cultural differences among its inhabitants.

The geographical conditions and the cultural variety among other things, have made it difficult to define the area. Nevertheless, there are as many similarities as there are differences within the numerous communities throughout the state. From this perspective, we have grouped the indigenous Oaxacans in various levels. The most well known grouping has been based on language, starting with the Zapotecs, Mixtecs, Mazatecs, Mixes, Chinantecs, Chatins, Chontales, Cuicatecs, Huaves, Zoques, Triques, Nahuas, Chochos, Amuzgos and the Ixcatecs.

A recent attempt at classification has been based on a regional division of Oaxaca in different areas with more detailed subdivisions. Thus we have a permanent exhibition of Oaxaca Ethnography here in the Anthropology Museum which divides the state into three schematic regions:

1. Zapotec region which includes two minor groups, the Chontales and the Huaves.
2. North Oaxaca which includes the Mixe, Chinantec, Mazatec and Cuicatec peoples.
3. Mixtec region which comprises five other groups the Chochotecs, Ixcatecs, Triques, Amuzgos and Chatinos.

DWELLINGS

There are a certain number of features common to all groups such as the fact that, all the settlements are scattered. The hamlets and dwellings are mainly scattered around the bigger towships and in the more lonely regions one can still see the traditional kind of housing. The building materials and shape may differ somewhat, according to the region but are generally a square room with plank or pole walls. Sometimes the latter are covered in mud (bajareque) in the mountainous regions or in the lower hotter regions. The roofs

Round huts or houses with cylindrical walls and conical roofs are typical of many coastal Mixtec families.

are either double sloped or pyramidal made of straw or another plentiful material in the area.

Among the traditional shapes found in the region is the typical housing of some the Mixtec and "mestizos" peoples of the coast. These are called "round houses" because they are circular with cylindrical walls and conical palm thatched roofs.

ECONOMY

The indigenous population of Oaxaca generally bases their economy on agricultural activities worked on either communal lands, privately owned, or inherited lands. This is complemented with gathering, fishing, arts and crafts and paid labor. The basic agricultural cultivation is maize, beans and pumpkin and, subject to the extent and fertility of the land produces in greater, or less quantity. There are very few small areas with some kind of irrigation which increases productivity. In the hot climate they cultivate a few commercial crops such as sugar cane, tobacco, coffee and some fruit-trees.

Farming technology varies according to whether it is in the vast majority of mountainous area or in the few flat areas. In the former, the old hand tools such as the hoe and planting stick are still employed and in the flat areas, plows and the occassional tractor are used.

In present day conditions, most families alternate various activities to achieve a subsistance level. Apart from the crops mentioned before, they gather wild fruits and vegetables and look after domestic animals such as chickens, pigs, horses or mules and cows or goats. Ocasionally they take paid jobs, particularly in the seasonal migrations to Sinaloa and Veracruz for tomatoe picking and sugar cane cutting. Those who are able, also migrate to the city to take third rate jobs in the city, day laborers, or shoe shine boys, etcetera.

In some places, they fish and make arts and crafts which include textile production, which to a certain extent, has been commercialized, especially women's clothing.

COMMERCE

Commerce is carried out in the weekly markets particularly in the "mestizo" towns in the varying areas. Large quantities of produce from a wide area brought in by different ethnic groups are concentrated in these markets.

RELIGION

Ritual and festive celebrations, organized through the wardenships which celebrate the cult to the Catholic images and advocations at the communal and family temples, are

of great importance. Likewise, celebrations such as saints days, christenings, confirmations, weddings, etc., are of great relevance.

It is commonplace that in such celebrations, hall dances, bull and wild horse riding and sporting events, take place. The latter include the Mixtec ball-game competition between the valley Zapotecs and the Sierra Mixtecs, which make up for a reminiscence of prehispanic games.

The appearance of protestant groups within the indigenous and "mestizo" groups is changing the traditional religious organization. This indoctrination has caused a division among the population and is disintegrating the indigenous culture.

One of the most beautiful regional dances of Mexico is the Feather Dance of the Zapotecs and Mixtecs in the Valley of Oaxaca.

POLITICAL STRUCTURE

The political structure has certain reminiscences of the prehispanic indigenous culture with a series of official positions in the municipal administration. Such is the case of the office held by the "topiles" or minor functionaries which still prevails.

ZAPOTEC REGION

The Zapotecs inhabit the central valleys of Oaxaca where the state capital is. The area extends along the Juárez Sierra and south to the Pochutla municipality where it borders with "Chatinos", the mixed negroid and Mixtec populations. They also inhabit the Tehuantepec Isthmus where they live in outlying villages with the Chontales, Huaves, Mixes and Zoques who have now been greatly influenced by the Zapotecs.

According to the 1980 census there is a population of 347,006 Zapotecs, which is the largest and most extensive indigenous group living in Oaxaca. Seventeen percent of these people speak only their native language and the rest are bilingual.

This party dress worn by the Zapotecs in the Isthmus is made of a black velvet *huipil* and *skirt* embroidered in exuberant multicolors.

ARTS AND CRAFTS

Among the better known commercialized crafts of the Valley is the green pottery from Santa María, Atzompa, the black pottery from San Bartolo Coyotepec and the red pottery from San Marcos Tlapazola. Also the blankets from Teotitlán del Valle, the woven belts from Santo Tomás Jalieza, the baskets from San Juan Guelavía, the grinding stones from Magdalena Teitipac and the leather and tin goods from Oaxaca city. One should also mention the clothing articles from the Zapotecs in the south of San Vicente Lachixio and San Antonio, the dresses from Yalalag of the hill Zapotecs and the dresses of the inhabitants of the Isthmus.

RELIGION

Large amounts of money go to pay for the ritual celebrations and festivals concerned with Catholic religious beliefs

A typical domestic scene in the Valley of Oaxaca where we see the type of *agricultural implements and the oven used to bake the green pottery of the region.*

and the local cult to the cycle of life. Particularly noticeable among these festivities, are the events that occur on the eve of the communal cult of carrying the saints in procession with alegorically decorated carts. The unmarried women, wearing beautiful floral arrangements on their heads take part in this procession. They also perform many dances among which, the most characteristic of the Valley is the Feather dance, the Gardeners dance and the masquerade of the Old men.

INDIGENOUS PEOPLE IN THE NORTH OF OAXACA

These are four ethnic groups that inhabit an area in the north of Oaxaca extending east and west in the Western Sierra Madre and include some lower regions on the Gulf side and some of the Isthmus planes reaching the Pacific side.

One of the distinctive cultural characteristic features of the indigenous Chinantec, Mixe and Mazatec communities in the north of Oaxaca, is the *female costume*.

178

The indigenous communities in the north of Oaxaca traditionally use *balsa wood canoes, half circle nets, dragnets, casting nets and "nazas" or traps,* for fishing.

These are the Cuicatecs, numbering 13,338 individuals, the 107,757 Mazatecs, the 66,811 Chinantecs and the 69,476 Mixes all speaking their indigenous languages according to the 1980 census. These languages belong to the Otomangue family with the exception of Mixe which has linguistic roots in Zoque-Maya.

FISHING

Fishing in this area is different from groups in the north of Oaxaca, particularly where there are great torrents of water such as in the Usila in the Chinanteca area. The traditional fishing techniques include rafts, canoes, oars, poles and various types of nets among which there are the half circle net, casting net and dragnets. The latter is distinguished by its rectangular shape woven with lead weights, and are sometimes as big as 24 meters long and 2 to 4 meters wide. They are used to catch larger fish such as the "bobo" and are handled by three of four fishermen.

The fishermen themselves have developed their own kind of dishes such as "shore broth", which they prepare on the banks of the river.

The building of reservoirs, particularly in the Mazatec and Chinantec regions, is an important fact that has inevitably affected the social and economic situation of the indigenous people. We particularly refer to the Miguel Alemán reservoir that was built in 1954 and the "Cerro de Oro" reservoir in the process of being built to regulate the waters of the Santo Domingo river.

All kinds of gourdes are used for domestic purposes among the Mixtecs of the coast.

RELIGION

Religious beliefs, still existing from prehispanic times include cults to certain natural elements such as rivers, mountains and caves. These are considered as being gifted with supernatural powers which man should try to control for his benefit. These cults are added to the beliefs around the Catholic saints and the rituals are performed by the "mayordomos" and automatically include the indispensable dance groups and music bands. The masquerade of the "Old Men" is one of the most characteristic dances organized by the Mazatec and Chinantec peoples. Whereas, the "Conquest" dances are more prominent among the Mixes localities and variations on the "Moors and Christians" dance with the dance of the "Negritos" and the "Tigers" dances.

Also notable among the local customs are certain magic-religious beliefs such as those related to the eating of *teonan-*

Following page. The most colorful male costume in Oaxaca is found among the *Tacuate* Mixtecs. It is embroidered with figures of animals and plants found in the region.

catl or hallucinary mushrooms. These are renowned to have therapeutic properties and are used to cure certain traditional illnesses such as the "the lost soul or spirit" when a person has been frightened in some place where the "owner of place" has taken possession of the soul of the person which can only be returned with the help of a healer.

MIXTEC REGION

Due to the geographical and cultural features of the Mixtecs, various attempts to regionalize them have been made, dividing the Oaxaca Mixtecs into three subregions: Lower Mixtec, Higher Mixtec or Sierra Mixtec and the Coastal Mixtecs. The Mixtec communities in the state of Puebla have been included in the Lower Mixtec and as the Mixtec people in the state of Guerrero intersect with Nahuas and Tlapanecas, have been called Nahua-Tlapaneca Mixtecs or the Mountain Region.

Living in the Mixtec region covering approximately 40,000 square kilometers, there are Mixtec speaking peoples with their varying differences, Spanish speaking "mestizo" people who are mixed races between Europeans, indigenous and negroid particularly in the coastal regions from the colonial period. Added to these, there are the minor ethnic groups such as the Triques, the Chocholtecs and Amuzgos who are Nahua speaking people particularly in Guerrero where they are mixed with Mixtec and Tlapaneco speaking people.

ARTS AND CRAFTS

Textiles and pottery are conspicuous among the arts and crafts of the region particularly the female garments and the clothes worn by male "tacuates". The region is noted for the pottery produced in Santo Domingo Tomaltepec and Santa María Cuquila, in the Mixtec Sierra, Jamiltepec and Coicoyan de las Flores, and in the Lower Mixtec, San Gregorio Silacayoapilla.

Woven palm items are produced in underground caves where the humid atmosphere softens the raw material so as to be able to weave easily.

RELIGION

Groups of pilgrims visit the sanctuaries or shrines at least once a year to fulfill promises or orders. They also offer petitions in the form of written words, personal objects (photos, hair, *ex-votos*, etc.), clay figurines, to ask their desire of the gods to cure illnesses, or obtain riches.

7. GULF OF MEXICO

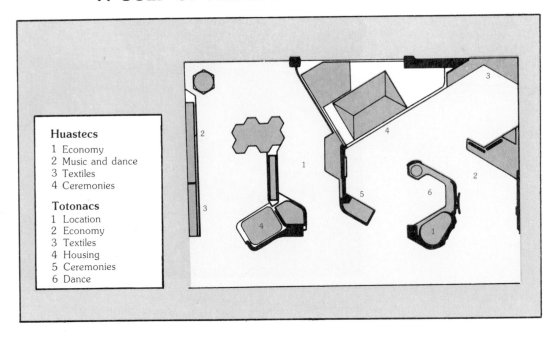

Huastecs
1 Economy
2 Music and dance
3 Textiles
4 Ceremonies

Totonacs
1 Location
2 Economy
3 Textiles
4 Housing
5 Ceremonies
6 Dance

THE TOTONACS

The Totonacs are located in the coastal plains of the state of Veracruz. The two most important settlements are the Totonacs in the Papantla region and those in the Jalapa-Misantla region.

Tropical climate prevails with rains in the summer, although in the winter, frosts are frequent in the villages situated in the higher lands.

The Totonac region is defined by the Cazones river in the north and the Antigua in the south. Other important rivers of the area include the Tecolutla, the Actopan, the Misantla and the Tecuantepec.

The Totonac language is of the Totonac family belonging to the Maya-totonac group with Totonac routes. There are various dialects which sometimes cause difficulty in understanding between the groups. These differences mainly occur in the Papantla and in the Jalapa-Misantla regions.

The main products of the area are maize, sugar cane and vanilla. Maize is sown in the early spring in cleared areas so that two crops a year can be obtained.

The economic importance of vanilla placed the Totonacs in a much more prosperous position than most of the other

indigenous people. However, the cultivation of vanilla in recent years has declined and many of the vanilla planters have been attracted elsewhere.

Some of the Totonacs live on their own allotments, but in general, most of the houses are grouped together near the hillside. In the Jalapa region the houses are practically touching each other in well defined streets. The public buildings are found in the center of the township.

COSTUME

The female dress in the Papantla region, is made of embroidered white organdy, consisting of a waisted skirt, blouse, *quechquémitl* and scarf. Few of the indigenous people of the Jalapa region still use their traditional dress.

The male costume consists of fine popelin, or cotton baggy pants and shirt. Some of the youngsters use brightly colored shirts. The men have lost the habit of waring their traditional clothes in the Jalapa-Misantla region, and have now adopted industrially made shirts and tousers; they also use boots, straw hats, machetes and shoulder bags.

DWELLINGS

The Totonac dwelling in the Papantla area is generally rectangular with a straw roof made of palm leaves or "misante-

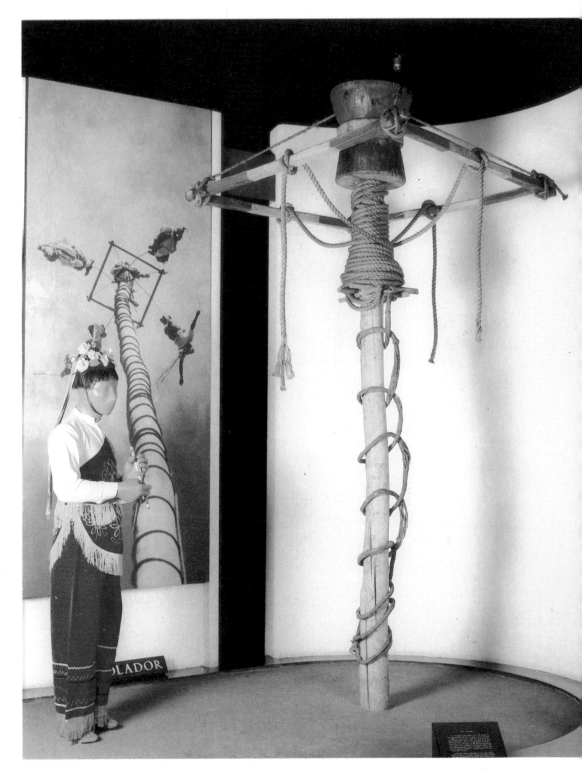

ca" leaves. The walls are made of vertical sticks and some are covered with mud. The house is usually one room which serves as kitchen, dining-room and sleeping quarters, although sometimes, a separate annex is built to serve as a kitchen. A loft to store maize is often found in the Jalapa area. All the houses contain domestic altars where the images and saints used in the family devotion are placed.

The native bee of the Papantla region is exploited to advantage. The honycombs are formed in hollowed out tree-trunks or pots hung in the shade of the outside wall of the house. The wax is used to make candles.

RITUAL CEREMONIES

Eight days after the birth of a child, a particular ritual is performed to curry favor with the "nanitas" or twelve old women. A special kind of "tamal" is prepared together with other food and licor. These and four candles are placed on a wooden box which serves as a table, where the midwife fumigates the objects related to the birth, with "copal" incense. Once the ceremony is over, the midwife makes a parcel of the "tamal" and other objects and leaves for the countryside with the father.

When someone dies in Papantla, the body is placed on a table with a lighted candle in its hands. Later when the body is moved to the coffin, it is accompanied by twelve miniature tortillas and reed grass with water. Ceremonies are performed for nine days following the death, and eighty days later and then a year after.

DANCES

Dances are among the most traditionally characteristic expressions of the Totonacs. All the main religious festivals are celebrated with dances, among which, the most well known are the "Guaguas", "Tocotines", "Huehues", "Volador", "Santiagueros" and the "Moors and Christians".

HUASTECOS

This group is situated in the north of the state of Veracruz and to the east of San Luis Potosí. With the exception of some higher prolongations of the Eastern Sierra Madre in the state of Veracruz, the region is flat. The climate is mainly tropical rainy where the principal rivers are the Pánuco and the Tamesí.

The Huastec language belongs to the Mayance group from the Maya-Quiché linguistic family.

Land ownership in the Huastec area is a complicated combination of communal and private lands

Women of the Huastec region weave on *waist looms* a loose textured material from "zapupe" fiber to make shoulder bags and other objects.

AGRICULTURE

The principal crops for home consumption are maize, beans, squash, yucca and sweet potatoe. Those produce for commerce are cane sugar, "zapupe", pineapples, bananas, oranges, mangos and coffee. Rough brown sugar is obtained from the sugar cane by a process of grinding, in animal-driven, wood sugar mills. The liquid runs through wooden containers to be collected in copper pans where it boils for three or four hours before it is turned into earthenware moldes for it to harden.

TECHNOLOGY

"Zapupe" is a fiber similar to henequen or sisal, and is prepared by cutting the leaves and removing the pulp through

There is a fairly large nucleus of Nahua people living in the Huasteca. The most important activity in *Chililico*, Hidalgo is making *pottery* where female hands produce a variety of pitchers, pots and toys of different shapes and sizes.

a defibering machine. The fiber is then wound round a stick which acts as a handle, and it is then put to dry on a platform. The fibers are twisted on a clapper of Spanish origin, called a *tarabilla* or *taranga*, which produces ropes and cords. Shoulder bags and other objects are also produced from "za-pupe". These are manufactured on the waist loom.

COMMERCE

Each important municipal township has one market day every week. Both the men and women sell their agricultural produce and the things they have made. Usually the women are the ones who sell fruit and tamales.

MUSIC AND DANCE

The Huastec have a musical tradition which still preserves some of the ancient musical instruments such as the flute, the drum, the *teponaxtli*, the rattle and the resonator. They also include the later instruments of the harp, the violin and the guitar. The characteristic dance of the Huastec region called the "huapango" is danced in pairs, either on a platform or directly tapped out on the dirth floor. The accompanying melodies and verses are sung as much in Spanish, as they are in Huastec.

The regional dances are the "Volador", also known as the "Eagle" or the "Hawk" dance, "Las Varitas" and the "Malinche".

COSTUME

The men wear rough cotton shirts and baggy pants, leather-thonged sandals or shoes, although recently, industrially made clothes have been introduced.

The dress of the Tantoyuca women is made at home with industrially produced materials even though in nearby villages the embroidered blouses and pleated skirts still persist. Female garb worn by the Huastecas in San Luis Potosí are flannel short skirts with a girdle, a cotton blouse or shirt, a *quechquémitl* and a scarf folded triangularly worn over the head, which is considered a luxury items. To complete the costume, the hair is generally braided with intertwined colored ribbons or yarn, to form a kind of crown known as *petob*. Sometimes the older folk use rattan to create this arrangement.

Detail of an embroidered Huastec *quechquémitl*.

189

INDIGENOUS MEDICINE

The medicine man of Aquismón can be of any age, but in Tantoyuca he is generally an old man. But in both places they say that the gift of healing is only passed down through very few families.

When the land is tilled ready for planting in Aquismón, an offering is made in the countryside. This consists of a large "tamal" or "bolim" the hearth of a chicken and "aguardiente".

During planting time a certain ceremony is performed in which twelve "dressed" corn cobs are placed on the family altar, a large tree is cut to make a sugar mill and an offering of "aguardiente", is made. In Aquismón a "bolim" or "aguardiente" offering is made to the tree when the mill is first used. The "aguardiente" is sprinkled in the four corners and all around the machine, and the heart of the chicken is burnt on the ground. The same rite is performed when house is used for the first time. However, in Tantoyuca, they also place palm crosses in each corner of the new house and offer a meal.

Among the agricultural rites performed by the *Huastecs* figures the *Ceremony to the new Maize* which takes place a few days before planting.

8. MAYAS OF THE LOWER REGIONS

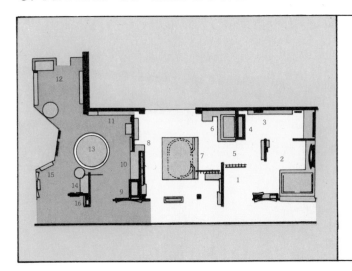

LOCATION

The Mayas of the Lower Regions inhabit a large geographical zone which integrates the states of Tabasco, Campeche, Yucatán, Quintana Roo and part of Chiapas.

The hidrography of the region varies and the state of Tabasco is where there are innumerable lakes, lagoons and extensive marsh lands. The two most important rivers of the region have their source in Guatemala and are called the Grijalva and the Usumacinta (sacred monkey). The flat terrain and permeability of the soil in Yucatán does not permit superficial rivers but there are abundant underground currents that have entrances to the surface called "cenotes".

LANGUAGE

The Maya linguistic family shows a complicated network of interrelationships difficult to unravel. It is probable that the languages presently spoken were part of an originally common linguistic family which through the years and for geographic and historical reasons changed little by little.

The Chol are in the state of Chiapas mainly in the Catazajá, Palenque, Salto de Agua, Tila, Tumbalá and Yajalón municipalities. Whereas the Chontal speakers inhabit the central part of Tabasco in the communities of Nacajuca, Centro Cintla, Jalpa and Macuspana. These people have two dialects, one in the coastal area, and Yocotán in Macuspana, where a large number of inhabitants speak the language.

The Lacandón Maya is divided into four different dialects; the Yucateco, Lacandón, Mopán and Itzá. The Yucateco

The Chontal dwelling is generally rectangular with no windows but with two doors opposite each other to create a draft of fresh air.

dialect is spoken in the states of Yucatán, Campeche and Quintana Roo.

HOUSING

Houses are rectangular shaped, with brick, plank or "bajareque" wattle walls, four sloping roofs with red tiles or thatched with palm leaf. If there are any beds, they are made of planks covered with rush matting but generally hammocks are used hung from the roof. A large trunk on top of a base takes up one side of the room; this trunk is the first gift that the woman gets when she marries. On the other side of the room, there is the "soul shrine" and next to it are the working tools such as the honey extractor, pails to take water to the fields and small stools to sit on. There are additions to the room such as a kitchen with a raised cooker, a *canché* or patch of land to sow culinary herbs, and apiary and a well which gets filled with rainwater.

ECONOMY

The Maya economy is based on maize and beans for home consumption but there are also commercial crops such as coffee, cocoa, "chicozapote" (fruit tree) and sisal. These are produced in plantations, orchards and inherited lands.

Chicle is also extracted in the area and often the Mayas are used for seasonal labor in the Campeche and Quintana Roo jungle. They are transferred to field camps mainly during the months from July to February.

The women, generally the wives, go to these camps to do the cooking and washing since the co-operative regulations do not permit the women to travel unaccompanied.

The "chicleros" (men who work the gum trees) extract the latex by making transversal cuts in the bark of the tree and place a paraffin soaked cloth bag underneath to collect the sap. This is cooked in cauldrons over a slow fire, after which it is taken to the co-operatives who send it to the international market.

Another of the basic crops harvested by the Maya, is sisal. The two plants most usually cultivated are the *zak-ki* or *Agave fourcroy-des lem* and the *Ya' ax-ki* or *Agave Sisilana Perrine*. Each plant yields about 2 to 3½% of its weight in fibre which is used to make various items which include bags and hammocks.

TRADITIONAL EXTRACTION OF HONEY AND BEESWAX

The beehives are found on tree trunks and when the honey is extracted, it is complete with honeycomb. This is squeezed

The Lacandones make use of all that nature offers: this *guitar* like musical instrument made from a gourd is a case in point.

The Lacandones live in temporary shelters "caribales" until the ground is used up when they move on the fresh lands. They use traditional costume for certain ceremonies.

193

Pottery is one of the oldest crafts. Here is an example of a piece made on a Prehispanic potters wheel or *kabal*. Some of the potters produce incensories, bowls and figurines for All Souls and All Saints Day. (or the "Day of the Dead")?

over a bucket so the honey remains crystalline. The wax is mixed with water and put to boil in a melting pan until it is liquid and left to cool so that the cake of wax can later be sold, or made into candles. The honey is taken to the monopolizers who export it to such places as Japan and other parts of the world.

HAT WEAVING

Among the outstanding crafts of the region is the manufacture of "jipijapa" (finely woven straw) hats. The finest of them all called "panamá", is woven with twenty-four straw threads. This activity is carried out in caves, in order to conserve the humidity and suppleness of the raw material.

CLOTHING

Each one of these groups has their own special way of dressing. The Chontal women wear a multi-colored embroi-

dered white blouse and a flowered cotton skirt. The Lancan-
dones wear long cotton *huipiles*. The Campeche
Mayas wear blouses embroidered with plant mo-

Among the home activities, the
Maya women make hammocks
and embroider.

tifs in black, with a skirt gathered at the waist, decorated with a lace flounce and a silk shawl. This dress is adorned with gold jewellery, either chains, rosaries and "salomónicas". They wear embroidered flat sandals on their feet.

The Yucatán Mayas wear what is called "mestiza costume" which consists of an embroidered petticoat called "fustán" under a *huipil* profusely embroidered with pumpkin flowers.

CEREMONIES

One of the most traditional ceremonies among the Mayas is the baptism of a child or *Hex mek*. The godfather carries the child astride his hip and takes nine turns round a table laden with objects pertaining to the future profession or employment of the boy child. For the girls, the main objects are still needles, threads and materials. The godfather will give the child money which expresses his desire that the child will never go penniless.

The religious festivals celebrated in the region take place in the village square and last nine days. There are typical dances every evening and the person in charge of the festivities takes a certain number of candles to the church, where they are distributed among the people who will be in charge the following year. One of them will be in charge of carrying the "pig's head" dancing all the way from the church to his house. Leading the way in front of the head is a person calling the pig with a gourd filled with maize. The festivities end in the house of the man carrying the head, with the "little bull" dance.

A very important agricultural ceremony of the region is that of the Chac-chac, which includes rites to propitiate rain and good harvests. It is carried out in the fields and only the men, accompanied by the community's Mayan priest or *H-men,* take part. Some children play the role of frogs, who call for rain during the ceremony.

DANCE

Among the Chontales of Tabasco, the dances are accompanied by a flute and a large, medium-sized and small drum. The drummers of Nacajuca are famous in the region for their interpretation of such traditional pieces as "La Gallina" (chicken), "El Tigre" (tiger), "El Baila Viejo" (the old trout) and "El Hombre Garrido" (the handsome man). The costume used in The Old Trout dance is distinctive in that the dancer uses a small mask on his face, a short sleeved shirt and "crossed over" pantaloons, and he holds a metal rattle and a semicircular fan in his hands.

Following page. Bridal and festive clothes are luxurious and are accompanied with gold filigree jewellery.

9. MAYAS IN THE UPPER REGIONS

The Tzotzil, Tzeltal, Tojolabal, Mame and Zoque Mayas live in the state of Chiapas. All their languages belong to the same Mayance roots.

ECOLOGICAL ENVIRONMENT AND SETTLEMENTS

Many of these communities are found near San Cristóbal de las Casas. Among the Tzotzil communities there is Larraínzar, Magdalena, Mitontic, Chamula, Zinacantán and Venustiano Carranza. The Tzeltales live in Bachajón, Tenejapa Oxchuc, Amatenango del Valle and Huixtan. The Tojolabales live near Comitán in Las Margaritas, La Independencia and La Trinitaria. The Mames live in La Grandeza and El Porvenir on the Guatemalan border and the Zoques have been moved to other communities near Tuxtla Gutiérrez after the eruption of the Chichonal Volcano.

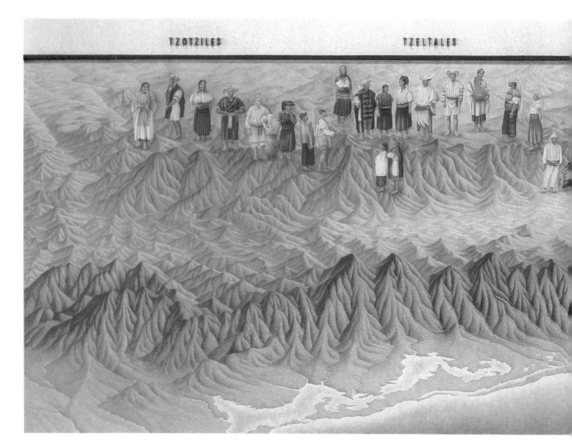

TZOTZILES   TZELTALES

The location of the indigenous communities in the hot lands or colder regions have caused changes. Those who live in the more isolated regions of the north are more conservative than those who live in the south near "mestizo" villages and have accepted many more changes.

Indigenous settlements are a group of houses or dwellings situated around a religious and political center where there is a church and a municipal administration in which the indigenous people take part and sometimes the "mestizos".

They all live in the same style houses with the only differences being in the building materials. They are one room dwellings divided into kitchen and bedroom and they have either pointed or ridged roofs. The furnishing is adapted to their necessities and now they frequently use plastic and spelter utensils in the kitchen.

POLITICAL AND RELIGIOUS ORGANIZATION

The indigenous communities are governed by two types of authority: the political, which follows the general pattern of the federal municipalities in which the majority of the offi-

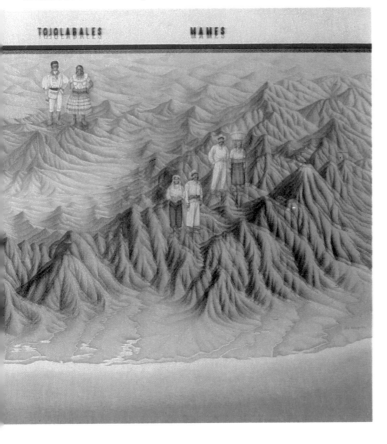

This map shows the *indigenous settlements*: the Tzotziles, the Tzeltales, the Tojolabales in the Highlands and the Mames on the Guatamalan border.

Among the Tzotziles, the men work in the fields, make baskets and carpentry while the women do the domestic work, spin and weave and some of them make pottery too.

cials are indigenous, with the paid secretary dealing with "paper work" being "mestizo", and the religious, which is based on both the Catholic and traditional rituals with "mayordomos", "capitanes" (leaders), lieutenants, aldermen and mayors. These officials have many obligations to fulfill, one of the most important being the organization of the festivities honoring the saints. The official positions are requested as a kind of penance. The leaders wear special garments and carry official batons. All the men of the community must fulfill the obligation to serve in some office without payment and it is fundamental to gain prestige. Many of the traditional characteristics are being lost because of contact with the "mestizos" or through the influence of other religions.

ECONOMY

The Maya diet is based on maize and its derivatives, such as el "pozol" (a kind of gruel) which is used on long journeys or when they go to the fields. Due to contact with the "mestizos" canned foods, alcoholic beverages and flavored soda waters have been introduced.

Sowing is carried out following the indigenous calendar, after the men have made petitions for rain and good harvests. Animals, irrigation and fertilizers are rarely used and the men still use the ancient hoes and planting sticks to sow the seed. During the season, the men go to the coffee plantations and the women remain to do all the work, looking after flocks of sheep and pig rearing which they trade for "aguardiente" (alcoholic beverage).

There is a large variety of manufactured goods which include textiles, woven bags, nets and baskets, saddlery and tannery, pottery, production of furniture and musical instruments such as harps and guitars.

Spinning and weaving are female activities and even though in some parts they have stopped producing textiles, it is still considered a family pride to wear the clothes made by their women folk. It is the women who prepare the wool, they wash it, teasel it, spin and dye it according to the piece of

Each community has introduced its own particular identifying variant on the traditional costume.
Tojolabal male.

clothing they are going to weave. However, they buy cotton thread and colored yarn.

Some communities, such as Chamula specialize in wool weaving, others, such as Venustiano Carranza specialize in cotton. Besides weaving, the women in other communities such as Tenejapa, Chenalhó and Magdalena make beautiful brocades and embroidery. In Zinacatán it is the custom to weave plumes into the edge of the wedding *huipil*.

There are few commercial activities among the Mayas themselves because they maintain a close commercial relationship with the "mestizos" buying from them objects for their rituals, materials, ribbons, tools, etc. in the large markets in San Cristóbal de las Casas and Comitán. However, the "mestizos" are always at an advantage in this relationship, when they sell their own products and when they buy from the indigenous people.

The production of "aguardiente" and "chicha" (popular fermented beverage) has now been severely restricted.

CLOTHING

The traditional costume is basically composed of the same garments, although each community has introduced their own particular variations. For example, different length shirts that become tunics in Oxchuc; short pantaloons with brocade at the leg in Tenejapa; short embroidered shirts of Zinacatán, heavy woollen jackets of Chamula, belts, leather-thonged sandals with heels, girdles, etc., the handmade shirts embroidered at the neck and sleeves of the Tojolabales and different shaped hats and brims with colored ribbon trimmings. These all vary depending upon how much contact they have with the "mestizos" and sometimes one now sees combinations with tennis shoes and industrial made shirts and pants.

Generally speaking, the women use a blue or black wool or cotton wound-around skirt with a woven or rough cotton embroidered blouse and handwoven *huipiles* with embroidered waists. The ones made in Chenalhó, Magdalena and Tenejapa are distinguished by their symbolic designs and those of Venustiano Carranza for their cotton brocades, where they also only use one skirt embroidered with colored "artisela". Other places are distinguished by their belts, headdresses or woollen shawls, the blankets used to carry babies or in the adornments. The Tojolabales wear hand-embroidered blouses, skirts trimmed with lace and a voluminous cotton underskirt and most of the women are barefooted.

The ceremonial costumes and those worn by the religious leaders are as elaborate as those worn by the dancers, who sometimes use velvet, little bells and animal-skin headdresses.

RELIGION

The entire Maya way of life is permeated with religion. They take many superficial rites and prayers from Christianity and their important festivals are on the day of the Patron Saint of the community.

The cross is venerated as the representation of God and is therefore found is all the houses, caves and dwellings. It is always decorated with flowers, incense and candles which are food to the gods. They use amulets to guard against the *nahuales* or evil spirit and as one can see, many of their beliefs have deep prehispanic roots, even the cult to the cross.

There is always plenty of food, drink, fireworks, music and dance in all the festivals. The most important are at Chistmas and carnival when, particularly in Chamula, they practice the rite of fire. This consists in setting alight a path of dry grass which has to be extinguished by running over it barefooted or with sandals. The change of authorities occurs in the New Year and is occasion for another fiesta. The San Caralampio festival that takes place in February in Comitán, is the most important festival for the Tojolabales.

In the more conservative communities, the custom is to pay for the brides wedding party and her new house. When she is about to give birth to a child, there are accompanying ceremonies, the most important being the "sowing of the soul". They believe that everyone has two souls: one which follows the way set out by the saints and the other which is eaten by the *nahuales* or evil spirits when he dies.

The local authorities and the mayordomos use their best clothes for ceremonies and festivals. *A second lieutenant from Chamula*

10. THE NORTHWEST

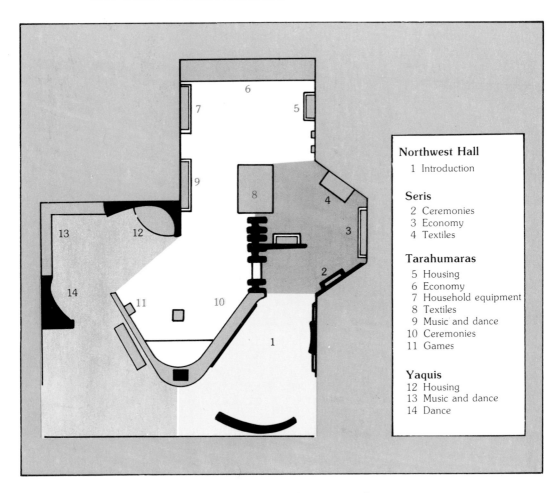

Northwest Hall

The northwest region of Mexico includes the states of Baja California, Sonora, Sinaloa and Chihuahua. It covers more than a third of the national territory, extending some 654 651 square kilometers. The typical climate of the northwest is dry and desertic or steppe land in the upper highlands. The Western Sierra Madre separates Chihuahua from the coastal plains and affords a variety of scenery within the region of mountains, deserts, coasts and valleys.

At the present time, fifteen ethnic groups live in this region, constituting a total population of more than 100,000 individuals. These are distributed in the following manner: five ethnic groups in Baja California: the Cucapá, Kiliwa, Cochimi, Pai-pai and Kumiai. The Pápagos, Opatas, Pimas, Jovas, Mayos, Yaquis, Seris and Guarijios live in Sonora and the Tarahumaras and Tepehuanos live in Chihuahua.

Fishing is one of the most important activities realized by the Seris because it affords the basis of their diet and is a source of economic income.

GEOGRAPHIC CONDITIONS

The three main components of the northwestern scenery are the sierra highlands, the coastal plains and the desert. The Western Sierra Madre runs the full length of the eastern part of this region, full of peaks and deep gorges with rugged terrain that causes enormous temperature changes and climatic conditions, ranging from snow capped peaks, coniferous forests to tropical ravines. Furthermore, heavy rains fall in the mountains, forming rivers carrying great volumes of water flowing down to the sea in long deep river beds.

There is an enormous plain in the coastal and central areas, furrowed by three great rivers, the Yaqui, Mayo and the Fuerte and innumerable streams. At the present time there are various reservoirs which control these waters and convert the area into fertile valleys suitable for commercial agriculture.

However, in contrast, in the north, the Sonora-Arizona desert is one of the most inhospitable deserts of the world, hot and dry with cactus and prickly scrub vegetation. The north part of the coastal plains adjoining the desert has its own physiographic characteristics with no important river running through the sothern part.

THE SERIS

The Seris inhabit the desertic stretch of the Sonora coast and the nearby islands. In recent years they have mainly settled in the two villages situated in desertic areas, Punta Chueca and Desemboque.

ECONOMY

The principal activities of the group are fishing, the making and selling of arts and crafts and food production. Secondary occupations include acting as tourist guides and helping in the rickety shops.

Usually the Seris go out on two to three day fishing trips and on the last day return to the coast for a few days before repeating the process. During the high tourist season some of these indigenous fisherman participate in the fishing around Bahía Kino, but during June and July fishing is practically nil.

These different types of vegetable fibre baskets made by the Seri women are called *coritas*.

At the present time the production of arts and crafts is the greatest activity and it is the men who fashion *figures in Palo de Fierro* (Iron wood).

The production of arts and crafts is an important activity within the indigenous group. The Seris manufacture four typical crafts at the moment, which are wood carving, basket weaving, rough cotton shirts and skirts, and shell necklaces.

SOCIAL ORGANIZATION

The group has been subjected to considerable change, particularly through the organization of a fishing co-operative and the introduction of new techniques and new jobs such as mechanics and carpentary. However, it is the local merchants and shipowners who benefit from the work of the Seris.

The Seri group have very poor living conditions, being without the most elemental urban services such as drinking-water, electric light and drainage. They also have a high index of illiteracy and insalubrity.

The belief in supernatural forces has declined considerably since the introduction of the Protestant religion, which has modified both the family and community way of life.

THE TARAHUMARAS

The word "Tarahumara" is a Spanish version of the indigenous word *Rarámuri* which means "light footed". The Tarahumara language comes from the Pimana family with yuto-nahua roots in the Nahua-Cuitlateco group and is an important element which helps preserve the group identity.

DEMOGRAPHY

There is a Tarahumara population of 60,000 people at the present time. These are scattered over an area of 60,000 square kilometers in 26 municipalities, which include Urique, Guachochi, Carichi, Bocoyna, Balleza, Batopilas, Morelos, Guadalupe y Calvo, Chinipas and Guazapares.

The basic population unit is a conglomoration of hamlets forming a village. The type of dwelling depends on the geographical characteristics. In the Tarahumara highlands there is plenty of wood so the houses are usually made from tree trunks, whereas in the lowlands they are made of stone and mud with thatch covered beams.

ECONOMY

This is a farming, hunting, gathering and sheep farming group whose agriculture is seasonal and only for home consumption. The produce cultivated in the Tarahumara highlands include maize, beans, wheat, pumpkin and potatoes,

The Tarahumaras weave *blankets and rugs* on horizontal looms supported on logs on the floor.

whereas in the lowlands as well as maize and beans, they also cultivate chile, oats and vegetables.

The most important arts and crafts are made from plant and mineral products and animal fibres such as wool, with which they make blankets and belts on hand looms.

SOCIAL ORGANIZATION

The Tarahumaras consider their traditional authorities their legitimate government. The *Siriame* or governor is elected by the people and is in charge of public order, justice and maintenance, according to the Tarahumara customs and values. They are assisted by military officials who include a general, various capitans, soldiers and policemen.

IDEOLOGY

The church is the religious and social center of the Christian Tarahumara communities and each village has its prayer teachers in charge of looking after the church.

209

The traditional ceremonies are related to an astral cult with fertility rites and ceremonies to drive away evil spirits or to invoke security and serenity. The Tarahumaras have beliefs in the sun and moon and in a great variety of malignant aquatic, subterranean and atmospheric beings.

DANCE

Dance is an important element in the Tarahumara lifestyle. it may be individual but frequently includes the family and others. They usually dance in a courtyard or open space before three crosses decorated with garlands and offerings. The *Tutuguri* is accompanied with magical chants and dances and the *Yumari* is a dance for the end of a festival, in which both the men and women take part led by a hunter. The "Matachines" dance was introduced during the colonial period and is performed in all the annual festivities using the most colourful costumes.

GAMES

The most usual games played are bowling races among the men, and races of throwing a small hoop among the women. The bowling races are formed of two teams each with their ball about the size of a baseball. They throw the ball as far as possible with their feet and the better runners let their companions tire so that they can join in at the end. They often bet with thread, wool, cotton cloth, mirrors and sometimes money and animals.

The *arihueta* game of the women is to throw an intertwined palm leaf hoop with a greased *coyajipari* stick. They also divide into two groups which decide on the starting and finishing point and the number of turns they have to make in the area which is shorter than the mens. They also wager bets.

THE YAQUIS

During 450 years the Yaquis have managed to become well known both in Mexico and the United States. Their profond sense of auto-determination and territorial sovereignty has pushed aside continual confrontations with various political authorities that have existed in the country since colonial times to the present day.

The Yaquis are located in an area of 4,890 square kilometers in the Guaymas, Cajeme, Bácum and Empalme municipalities of the state of Sonora. They form a defined political and territorial unit with specific population nuclei. Therefore each community may be composed of several groups:

Following page. Chapayeka or Pharisee mask of the type used in the Passion plays which represent harmful beings.

the Cócorit, Bácum, Torim, Vícam, Róhum, Huírivis, Pótam and Belén. The climate in this semidesertic region is extreme, sometimes registering temperatures of 40°C in summer and 3°C in winter.

ECONOMY

The customary crops are beans, pumpkins, maize and others which have been substituted by wheat, cotton, sesame seed, chickpea and soya. With official support a fishing co-operative was created in 1980 and a further cattle raising co-operative was formed in 1982. Apart from the agricultural, fishing and cattle raising organizations, there are others which gather together a lesser number of members.

The arts and crafts manufactures by the Yaqui complement their agricultural activity. The main craft is rush matting. Pharisee masks, rosaries and grotesques masks for the "pascola" dances and musical instruments are made specially for those in charge of the festivities.

SOCIAL ORGANIZATION

The villages which also include their corresponding lands, form the basis of the territorial organization of the Yaqui society. Each village has their civil, military and religious institutions which unite to organize the social life of the Yaquis. The civil institutions take place in a village assembly in which every member takes part. There is an elder called the "village mayor" and a group of governors. The military institution is made up of different ranking individuals from soldiers to captains, and the organization is based on the three main institutions of the church, festivals and traditions.

MUSIC AND DANCE

Music and dance are particularly important among the Yaqui and there is not a single ceremony or festivity that does not include music and dancers. There are three groups of dancers with their respective musicians and singers who are in charge of satisfying this social demand: Deer Dancers, "Pascola" dancers and the "Matachine" dancers.

11. THE NAHUAS

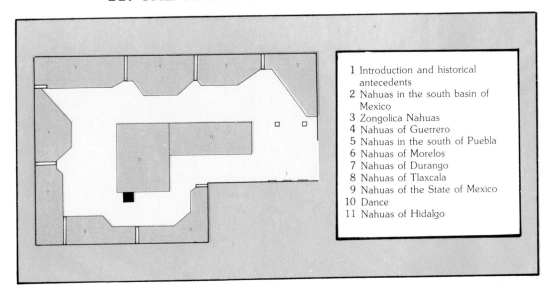

The most widespread group of indigenous people in the living in Mexico today is the Nahuas. We find settlements in thirteen places throughout the country: Puebla, Hidalgo, Veracruz, Morelos, San Luis Potosí, Guerrero, Jalisco, Durango, Tlaxcala, Oaxaca, State of Mexico, Colima, and the Federal District. In the 1980 General Population Census there was a population of 1,376,989 Náhuatl speaking inhabitants.

To understand why this population is so dispersed, we have to go back to prehispanic times. Some of the Nahua groups emigrated to their present location, first of all with the fall of Tula, and later due to other political and economic events.

It was the Mexica lords who began to expand the Mexico-Tenochtitlán dominions through a series of military and economic conquests throughout the Mesoamerican territory. These conquests imposed a domination that was reflected in paying tributes. Influence was exercised over the leaders to adopt Nahua ways, superimposing Náhuatl names to their villages. Náhuatl became the most important Mesoamerican language and even extended into Central America where we still find Náhuatl village names in Nicaragua, Honduras, and El Salvador.

The Spanish conquest increased the dispersion of the Náhuatl population by transporting large numbers from Tlaxcala to colonize extensive areas in the north of the country. This is how towns such as Santa Fe, San Esteban de la Nueva Tlaxcala, and San Antonio de Béjar were founded. These colonizers took with them their language and many cultural patterns. Remnants of these are still found in the popular dances of Zacatecas, Coahuila, and Nuevo León, particularly the dance of the "Matachines". This is also the reason why the textile industry flourished in Coahuila. Due to the Spanish invasion, some of the Nahuas took refuge in the more inaccessible places, such as the high mountains where the Spaniards had no incentive to settle, because there were no mining, agricultural, or cattle raising possibilities on a larger scale. These regions remained isolated from Spanish influence until the late sixteenth century. These communities were incorporated much more slowly into the new systems than were the Nahuas who lived nearer the larger colonial towns.

Now the Nahuas inhabit a great variety of different ecological zones due to their wide dispersion. They are all basically country farmers who have resolved their production problems in a variety of ways according to their particular situation. The basic crops of maize, beans, coffee and sugar cane are cultivated accordingly and are complemented with further agricultural produce.

We have displayed the most important aspects of the Nahua culture in this hall. Here we have shown the Nahuas from the Federal District, Veracruz, Hidalgo, Guerrero, the Puebla Sierra, Morelos, Durango, Tlaxcala, and the State of Mexico. Certain aspects of the traditional costume and language have been lost in some of these areas, but nevertheless the identifying Nahua cultural patterns have been preserved mainly in the religious ceremonies and dances.

The Nahuas in the Zongolica hills Veracruz, use waist looms to weave the traditional woollen ponchos proudly worn by the men.

214

The Huastecs who are producers of items made of "zapupe" and palm fibre are frequently seen selling their ware of *hats, belts and bags*, in the Nahua market of Huejutla, Hidalgo.

FEDERAL DISTRICT

ECONOMY AND AGRICULTURAL PRODUCE

The boroughs of Xochimilco, Tláhuac and Milpa Alta are situated in the south of the Federal District and these have preserved a Nahua population up until the present time. They fulfil an agricultural role vitally important to the City of Mexico. The "chinampas", are man-made floating pieces of land planted with vegetable gardens with a high agricultural production of food supplying the metropolitan area. Unfortunately, enormous areas of Tláhuac and Xochimilco that were previously used for agriculture, have now been built up into urban areas. This has contaminated the area more and more, and the ecological deterioration is considerable. The water level necessary to preserve the chinampas

215

has diminished considerably, the springs have dried up and some of the city wastes drain into the canals. As a consequence, vegetable produce has fallen and is now insufficient to satisfy the local needs.

CENTRAL VERACRUZ

ECONOMY AND AGRICULTURE

Since the end of the nineteenth century the greatest number of Nahuas inhabiting the central part of Veracruz now cultivate coffee, mainly in their own small allotments. They still use traditional methods for planting coffee underneath enormous trees that protect them from the frost. The coffee harvest begins in November and the picking season increases in January and February. Immediately after harvesting, the coffee beans are dried on rush matting in the back yards of the houses where it is turned over several times a day to dry out thoroughly. Then the beans are separated in elaborate crushing mills that have been used since the beginning of the nineteenth century. The beans obtained by this method are either stored in sacks or "tenates" for home consumption, or are sold in small quantities to the monopolies.

Coffee goes through a long process of commercialization, starting with the farmers who produce it to the transnational companies who buy it up in large quantities. Maize has never stopped to be sown in the region; this crop has a substantial meaning in the natives' daily nourishment.

HIDALGO

This is the state in which the greatest number of Náhuatl speaking people live, mainly in the Huasteca region, including twelve municipalities around Huejutla.

ECONOMY

Commerce has been an important activity in this region since prehispanic times. The regular street markets allow the farmers to exchange their goods from hunting, gathering and harvesting. The women offer all kinds of cooked foods, pottery and textiles. During the colonial period commerce was monopolized by peninsular Spaniards but they allowed the indigenous people to continue with their street markets.

Now the Huejutla market is an economic institution in charge of organizing the distribution of goods between

producers and consumers from a wide area. Commercial activity fluctuates within the weekly cycle. Saturdays start the greatest activity since a considerable number of roving vendors come into town for the Sunday street market. These come from forty three different villages around Huejutla. A large number of Nahua women from Chililico live in the town itself and they sell their pottery wares. People come from great distances, even from the center of Mexico, from Tantoyuca with "zapupe" fiber products, and from Platón Sánchez.

GUERRERO

The Nahua group in this state live in very precarious conditions, as shown by the high unemployment figures, low income levels, insufficient services, deficient nourishment, illiteracy, injustice, and oppression.

ECONOMY AND FAMILY INDUSTRY

The economy of the group is based on seasonal agriculture, cultivating the most important crop which provides the basic food for the population: maize. Every member of the family contributes with his work to help supplement their income. These activities include pottery, decorating gourds, bark paper, other wood materials, and the weaving of palms. In some regions the women weave and embroider their

The best known craft of the Nahuas from the central Balsas region is *painting on bark paper*.

costumes, such as in Acatlán. In other places, the family dedicates itself to selling stone and wooden objects, such as in Xalitla.

PUEBLA SIERRA

TRADITIONAL MEDICINE

Nowadays, there are various specialists among the Nahuas who, according to their specialty, are called herbalists, midwives, chiropractors, bonesetters, faith healers, fortune tellers, healers and medicine men. There are also witch doctors, or spell casters who are sometimes confused with the healers probably because from prehispanic times it was known that "el que hechiza sabe también como quitar el hechizo" (the one who casts the spell knows how to lift it also) and many times the same person fulfills the two functions. The healers have a wide knowledge of the medicinal properties of plants, minerals, and animals, which are used in various forms of infusions, ointments, and poultices for the curing of illnesses.

This medicine has been called "traditional medicine" and is deeply rooted in most of the ethnic groups. It is a medicine that is officially ignored of set aside, despite the fact that the vast majority of Mexicans in both the century and in urban areas practice it daily.

The Nahua "chamanes" (medicine men) of Huauchinango have a special ceremony on the first day of the year called the "Big Flower". They make offerings of chocolate, bread, tamales, chicken, paper, candles, "aguardiente" (strong, alcoholic beverage), and flowers to the *yiyantlis* or *mesas* in a place where the vapors dwell, and in caves or sacred places.

MORELOS

RELIGION

A minority of the large farming population found in the state of Morelos still speak Náhuatl. However, despite the cultural changes that they have suffered, the majority of the Morelos population still preserve very definite indigenous cultural features. An example of this is the flowering or "periconeada" ceremony performed throughout Morelos on the morning of September 28th, the day before the "arrival" of Saint Michael on the 29th.

DURANGO

There is a small nucleus of Nahuas in Durango known by the name of Mexicaneros who live with the Tepehuanes and other groups.

The Mexicaneros call the "mitote" or dance festivities the *Xurawet*. In this ceremony they petition mainly for rain. The festival takes place in the main square of the ceremonial

On the first day of the year, medicine men in the North Puebla Sierra, perform a ceremony in the surrounding caves, when offerings are made of bread, chocolate, candles and what is known as *Flor Grande*.

*Left. The Tlacoloieros dance is
related to maize cultivation and
represents the difficulties
encountered by the peasants in its
production.*

*Right. The Chinelos of
Tlayacapan and Tepoztlán in the
state of Morelos, wear beautiful
velvet costumes and enormous
headdresses called "Cubetas", in
the carnival celebrations.*

center of the Mexicanero capital, Pedro Xícora. Sometimes
it also takes place in the private yards of the surrounding
hamlets.

They perform the *Xurawet* ceremony in May to call for
the rains. The fields are tilled for sowing and the mayor and
his assistant are in charge of the purification while the entire
population fasts. The mayor, first of all, talks to the gods
or patrons, he cries out for his people, he dreams of times
to come, and leads the "Feather dance" and the "Deer dance".
Both men and women join in and the assistant mayor taps
out the different rhythms for the dances on a "jícara" (hollow
gourd).

The Mexicaneros put flowers and tamales for the gods
on the altar, and they tie feathers to the arrows which carry
their supplications.

DANCE

Man has found a medium to express his emotions, beliefs,
and personality in dance. It reflects not only artistic aspects
but also complex ways to interpret the world and reality.

The Nahua Hall displays five typical costumes used in the
dances and shows some of the richness in the indigenous

Nahua traditions. Here we can compare the differences and similarities between the costumes used by the "paragüeros" of Tlaxcala with their moveable eyed masks and European style dresses; and the Tlaxcala "charros" with their embroidered, spangled capes and hats decorated with feathers. The typical "Tlacololero" dance of Guerrero maintains a tradition linked to agriculture and man's fight with nature. The well known "Chinelos" from Morelos and the "Sonajeros" from Jalisco are different dance forms surviving in regions that otherwise have lost many of their indigenous customs, such as the language and costume.

TLAXCALA

ECONOMY AND FAMILY INDUSTRIES

Blankets and rugs are manufactured in the state of Tlaxcala and are generally made of wool. This tradition dates from the colonial period when the Spaniards introduced the pedal loom to weave the materials used for their own dress. The indigenous people learned to use it and to work with new fibers such as the wool and linen indispensable in Span-

Left. The men of Tuxpan, Jalisco use special costumes to dance *the Sonajero dance*, named after the rattle instrument held in the hands.

Right. During the *Xurawet* ceremony of the Mexicaneros in Durango, the Deer dance is performed.

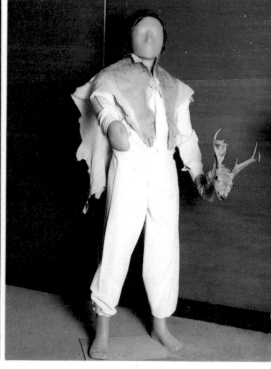

ish garments. The men work the pedal loom while the women spin the wool and perform other processes necessary to the textile industry.

STATE OF MEXICO

The Nahuas in the State of Mexico have been subjected to great cultural changes mainly due to the enormous influences of the urban and industrial environment emanating from Mexico City. Mass communication of radio, newspapers and television has had a lot to do with the change, and although many still work in the fields, many have become manual laborers, vendors and small-time craftsmen.

The women perform domestic work either in their own houses or in the urban areas surrounding Mexico City. They also make clothes, particularly weaving woollen garments which are sold in Chiconcuac.

Bibliography

ARIZPE LOURDES **Parentesco y economía en una socie-**
dad nahua México, INI, 1973.
"De la tierra a la industria: migración y organización social actual de los nahuas". **En Primera Reunión sobre**
Estudios antropológicos de los nahuas. México, julio,
1984.

AVELEYRA ARROYO DE ANDA, LUIS MANUEL MALDONA-
DO KOERDELL y PABLO MARTINEZ DEL RIO. "Cueva
de la Candelaria". **Memorias del INAH**, SEP, Vol. I México, 1956.

BARLOW, ROBERT H. "Resumen de la historia Tolteca". **This**
Week. 1948.

BEALS RALPH, HOIJER HARRY. **Introducción a la Antro-**
pología. Ediciones Aguilar. Madrid, España. 1969.

BELL, BETTY (editor). **The Archaeology of West Mexico**.
Sociedad de Estudios Avanzados del Occidente de México, Ajijic. 1974.

BRAMBILA PAZ, ROSA M. **Teotihuacán**. G.V. Editores, México, D.F. 1984.

CARDOS DE MENDEZ, AMALIA. **Los Mayas**. G.V. Editores,
México, D.F. 1984.

COMAS, JUAN. **Introducción a la Prehistoria General**. Di-
rección General de Publicaciones. Instituto de Historia.
Universidad Nacional Autónoma de México. México,
1962.

DAHLGREN, BARBRO Y OTROS. "Huastecos, totonacos y
sus vecinos" en **Revista Mexicana de Estudios Antro-**
pológicos T. XIII, Núms. 2 y 3. México, 1953.

DEPARTAMENTO DE ETNOGRAFÍA. **Guía de Salas de Et-**
nografía. Museo Nacional de Antropología. INAH, México, 1984.

DI PESO, CHARLES. **Casas Grandes** (8 volúmenes) A Fallen trading-center of gran chichimeca. The Amerind Foun-
dation inc./Dragoon Northland Press./Flagstaff. 1982.

DINERMAN, INA R. **Los tarascos: campesinos y artesanos**
de Michoacán, SEP (Colección SepSetentas, 129). México, 1974.

DISKIN, MARTÍN SCOTT COOK. **Mercados de Oaxaca**. INI,
México, 1975.

GARCIA VALENCIA HUGO. **Sala del Golfo** en una visión
del Museo Nacional de Antropología. 1979.

GONZALEZ RODRIGUEZ, LUIS **Tarahumara la sierra y el**
hombre. SEP/80 México. 1980.

LASTRA, YOLANDA. "Las áreas dialectales del náhuatl mo-
derno" en **Primera Reunión sobre estudics Antropoló-**
gicos sobre los nahuas. México, julio, 1984.

LOPEZ AUSTIN, ALFREDO. **Tarascos y mexicas** RCE México, 1981.

LUMHOLTZ CARL. **El México Desconocido**. Editora Nacional T. II Reimpresión. México, 1972.

NOLASCO ARMAS, MARGARITA. **Notas para la antropo-**
logía del Noroeste. INAH, México, 1969.

OLIVER VEGA BEATRIZ. "Los grupos otomianos" **Cuader-**
no de trabajo No. 2. Sección de Etnografía M.N.A. INAH
México, 1974.
"La Sierra de Puébla" en **Una visión del Museo Nacio-**
nal de Antropología. México, INAH, 1979.

PADDOCK, JOHN **Ancient Oaxaca**. Stanford University
Press, Stanford, California, 1966.

PIÑA CHAN, ROMAN. **Las culturas preclásicas de la Cuen-**
ca de México. Fondo de Cultura Económica. México,
1955.
Una visión del México Prehispánico. Instituto de Inves-
tigaciones Prehispánicas. UNAM. México, 1967.

ROSELL DE LA LAMA, GUILLERMO. "Tula" **Estados tolte-**
cas eran ciertamente sabios, solían dialogar con su
propio corazón. Gobierno del Estado de Hidalgo. México, 1980.

RUZ, ALBERTO **El pueblo Maya**. Salvat mexicana de Ediciones, S.A. de C.V., 1981.

SCHONDUBE, OTTO. "El Occidente de México hasta la épo-
ca tolteca", **Historia de México**, Vol 1 Salvat Editores,
México, 1974.

THOMPSON, J. ERIC S. **Grandeza y decadencia de los ma-**
yas. Fondo de Cultura Económica, México.

TRANFO, LUIGI. **Vida y Magia en un pueblo otomí del Mez-**
quital INI SEP. México D.F. 1974.

VILLARROJAS, ALFONSO. **Notas sobre los huicholes**. Pla-
neación e Instalación del Museo Nacional de Antropolo-
gía. INAH, CAPFCE, SEP. 1961.
Los mayas de Tierras Rojas. Capfce. DIMNA, SEP
INAH. México, 1962.
Los mayas de las Tierras Altas México, CAPFCE, DIM-
NA, SEP-INAH. (mimeográfiado) 1964.
"Los elegidos de Dios". **Los mayas de Quintana Roo**.
INI México D.F. 1971.

VOGT, EVON, Z. Ed. **Los zinacantecos. Un pueblo tzotzil**
de los Altos de Chiapas. México, SEP - INI. 1966.
Handbook of Middle American Indians. "Ethnology",
Robert Wauchope Gen. Ed. University of Texas Press.
Austin Vols. 7 y 8, 1969.

WAUCHOPE, R. (edit. Gral.) **Handbook of Middle Ameri-**
can Indians. Vol. 1 "The Patterns of farming Life and
Civilization" p. 446-498. University of Texas Press, Austin. USA. 1964.

WHITECOTTON, JOSEPH W. **Los zapotecos, príncipes, sa-**
cerdotes y campesinos. Fondo de Cultura Económica,
México, 1985.